D1496420

Celebrating
Sunday
Evening
Prayer

CELEBRATING SUNDAY EVENING PRAYER

A Resource for Parishes
and Communities

Liturgy Office of the Catholic Bishops'
Conference of England and Wales

Canterbury Press Norwich

First published in 2006 by the Canterbury Press Norwich
(a publishing imprint of Hymns Ancient & Modern Limited,
a registered charity)
St Mary's Works, St Mary's Plain,
Norwich, Norfolk, NR3 3BH

www.scm-canterburypress.co.uk

Liturgy Office, Catholic Bishops' Conference of England and Wales,
39 Eccleston Square, London SW1V 1PL

www.liturgyoffice.org.uk

British Library Cataloguing in Publication data

A catalogue record for this book is available
from the British Library

ISBN-10: 1 85311 732 3
ISBN-13: 978 1 85311 732 9

Cover design by Leigh Hurlock
Calligraphy by Ewan Clayton
Music engraving by Andrew Parker

Designed and typeset in Quadraat
by Simon Kershaw at crucix www.crucix.com

Printed and bound in Great Britain
by William Clowes Ltd, Beccles, Suffolk

Contents

Contents

Foreword

Introduction

Resources

Appendices

FOREWORD

In the liturgy we are invited to share in Christ's prayer, offering divine praise to the Father and interceding for the salvation of the whole world. The liturgy takes many forms, but its two most regular expressions are the celebration of the Eucharist and the celebration of the Liturgy of the Hours.

The importance of the Eucharist is clearly understood in our parishes, and much has been done in recent times to ensure that this sacrament is celebrated reverently and fruitfully.

In the years since Vatican II many parishes have also become familiar with the revised form of the Liturgy of the Hours (The Divine Office). Thirty years ago or so, this liturgy was seen as pretty much the preserve of the clergy and the religious. Now it is prayed by many lay people individually and it features more and more often in the regular timetable of parish communities.

Celebrating Sunday Evening Prayer will build on this progress and help the Church in England and Wales to respond to the call of the Fathers of the Second Vatican Council that on Sundays and the more solemn feasts every effort should be made for the celebration in common and in church of the Liturgy of the Hours, and especially Vespers.

Informed by good practice around the dioceses of England and Wales, this volume puts flesh on the proposals in the *praenotanda* to the Divine Office as to how the standard pattern of the Liturgy of the Hours can be adapted for worthy celebration in common. The guidance and resources it offers will help those preparing and leading these celebrations to ensure that they offer a richness of symbol, text and music appropriate to the dignity of the liturgy, and capable of nourishing the prayer and devotion of the faithful gathered in Christ.

+Arthur Roche
Bishop of Leeds

Chairman of the Department for Christian Life and Worship
Catholic Bishops' Conference of England and Wales

INTRODUCTION

You are a people set apart to sing the praises of God,
who called you out of darkness into his wonderful light.

1 PETER 2:9

Christians have always marked the morning and evening hours of the day with prayer. The earliest sources outside the New Testament tell us that they prayed the 'Our Father' at morning and evening. Other early documents tell us that they blessed the lighting of lamps at the hour of sunset by calling on Christ, the 'joyful light' of God the Father.

We know that by the time Christians were able to practise their religion freely – the fourth century – the traditions of public morning and evening liturgy were well established.

Morning Prayer was a service of thanksgiving and praise to God, offered in and through Christ. With each new dawn it recalled Christ's resurrection and our sharing in this new life. Psalms and hymns were sung and the prayers of intercession looked forward to the day ahead, asking God's blessing on its concerns.

Evening Prayer on the other hand looked back and thanked God for the blessings of the day that was passing. It remembered Christ's death and our Christian call to die with him to sin and to live in holiness. Thus the whole of the day was encompassed within the death and resurrection of Christ – the paschal mystery through which we are redeemed. Evening Prayer celebrated the arrival of dusk by the lighting of lamps and candles. Incense was often burnt as a penitential rite, something that linked with the 'evening sacrifice' of Christ on the cross. Intercessions and prayers brought in the world and all humankind into the mystery of Christ, our light.

Liturgy is public worship – the very word comes from *leitourgia* meaning *work of the people*. It is the communal celebration of God's work of salvation in Jesus Christ. It is ritual celebration which of its nature demands more than words. These liturgies were for the whole Church; they were colourful and action centred. As well as lighting lamps and burning incense, people moved around the church, pausing at the font, the cross, special relics and so on. Something of this still lives on when, for instance, we celebrate the Way of the Cross as a procession around the church, or the Taizé custom of Friday evening 'Prayer around the Cross'.

These liturgies were acts of worship for everyone, not just clergy, but celebrated regularly in the big city churches built at the time by the whole community of the Church: bishop, priests and people.

With the growing importance of monastic life, the style of prayer changed. It became more word-centred, more a meditation on the psalms and scripture, less of a ritual action: (psalms recited one after the other, the whole 150 in one week; the whole bible once each year and so on). This was the style of 'office' (literally 'duty') that later became the 'breviary' of the priest. Its character as liturgical celebration was diminished.

Even so, some 'people's' liturgy remained: Sunday Vespers, once common at least in Europe; the very popular 'Compline' last thing at night, and so on. Other 'Devotions' came in too, with the growing cult of the Blessed Sacrament. These things provided the colour and popular sentiment once associated with Lauds and Vespers.

The Second Vatican Council wanted to restore to the people something of the daily, popular liturgy, morning and evening. The great 'Constitution on the Sacred Liturgy' which set in motion the reform of the Roman Rite, wrote of this form of prayer:

> Pastors should see to it that the chief hours, vespers particularly, are celebrated in common in church on Sundays and the more solemn feasts.
>
> SC 100

'The chief hours': this type of liturgy is bound up with the passage of time. The 'hour' is a great biblical theme: the hour of salvation, Jesus' 'hour' of glorification in St John's Gospel, etc. These hours are the pivots of the day: darkness into light, light into darkness. They may be also the 'hour' of God's redeeming grace, when at morning he is named as Life, the Sun of Justice rising from death or at evening, as Light of the world, the true evening sacrifice.

This brief survey has been given not to recapture a golden age and resuscitate it, but rather to enable us to know and respect the tradition we have inherited and refashion it in a way which is valid for our own time. As the *General Instruction on the Liturgy of the Hours* says:

> The liturgy of the hours is not seen as a beautiful
> memorial of the past demanding intact preservation
> as an object of admiration; rather it is seen as open to
> constantly new forms of life and growth and to being the
> unmistakable sign of a community's vibrant vitality.
>
> GILH 273.

If this is to be realised, parish communities will need to be open to the principles outlined in paragraphs 33 and 279 of the same Instruction, where it says respectively:

> In a celebration in common and in private recitation the
> essential structure of this liturgy remains the same, that
> is, it is a conversation between God and his people. Cel-
> ebration in common, however, expresses more clearly the
> ecclesial nature of the liturgy of the hours; it makes for
> active participation by all, in a way suited to each one's
> condition, through the acclamations, dialogue, alter-
> nating psalmody and similar elements.
>
> GILH 33

> The main consideration is to ensure that the celebration
> is not too inflexible or elaborate nor concerned merely
> with the formal observance of rules, but that it matches
> the reality of what is being celebrated. The primary aim
> must be to inspire hearts with a desire for genuine prayer
> and to show that the celebration of God's praise is a thing
> of joy.
>
> GILH 279

Respecting the principles in both these quotations, parishes can develop a form of morning and evening prayer which is authentic and meaningful to those who celebrate.

Here are some aims for a parish celebration – that it be:

- *a liturgy of time*: we celebrate the passover moments symbolised in the transfer from dark to light and light to dark.
- *simple in outline*: the structure should be clear and the patterns of prayer respected.
- *ritual prayer rather than read text*: create a worthy and inviting environment; sing the psalms and hymns; use symbol, gesture and movement.
- *shared by all*: distribute the ministries as widely as possible and involve people in the preparation.
- *constant*: this prayer speaks of God's fidelity and of the Church's effort to be faithful in responding to God in Christ. Better a little each Sunday than an occasional flourish. The rhythm of morning and evening prayer will grow in us and enrich our parishes as it punctuates our lives.
- *open*: Morning and Evening Prayer has been celebrated in some form by all the churches throughout the centuries. It is a liturgical celebration which can bridge the denominational divide and be a worthy and authentic expression of our common baptism into Christ.

> Let the word of Christ dwell in you in all its fullness,
> as you teach and counsel each other in all wisdom by
> psalms, hymns, and spiritual canticles, singing thankfully
> to God in your hearts.
>
> COLOSSIANS 3:16

The Assembly and its environment

All Christian worship begins with the gathered community of the Church which we call the assembly. It is the primary symbol of Christ present in and with us, so that we all may be one.

In our buildings for worship the needs of the community are reflected in the spatial arrangements. The focal points of altar, ambo and chair show us the action of the eucharistic celebration: the font points out the importance of initiation. When we consider the prayer of the church we find that this does not fit easily into the space arranged for sacramental celebration, it needs its own shape to bring out its significance.

Gathering

Depending on circumstances practical suggestions might include:

- the use of a separate chapel or space within the building;
- the rearrangement of a small area of the worship space: seats facing inwards, a horseshoe arrangement, or perhaps grouped together in a less formal manner;
- using the main worship space or a large sanctuary but trying to focus on the community, not on elements associated with sacramental worship.

The shape of the arrangement needs careful thought. Whilst there is no *ideal* solution, the symbol of gathering suggests some form of circular or *choral* setting, e.g., facing one another.

Whatever space you prepare consider the following:

- enough seating and ease of access;
- provision for the different ministries: reader, musician;
- the physical objects of worship: candle, incense bowl;
- lighting;
- amplification (if necessary).

It is important that the congregation is comfortable with the arrangement and feels part of the liturgy. The celebration of the liturgy of the hours requires a model of worship that allows for a greater flexibility in ministry and roles.

Symbol

Various symbols are associated with Evening Prayer. The ones listed have a long and ancient history in Christian worship.

Light

The associations of light with the liturgy are many and varied: Christ our light, the resurrection, the baptismal candle, the celebration of Candlemas and so forth. The kindling of lamps as evening fell became a reminder of Christ our light which in turn provided the lucernarium rite. The group may choose to have one centrally placed candle (in the Easter season the Paschal Candle) or a variety of smaller ones according to the festivity providing we remain true to the tradition of a living flame, thus excluding false and artificial candles.

Incense

Following scripture and the tradition of the Church incense has been used as a sign of oblation for the protection and blessing of God. At the evening office it was used as a sacrificial offering – prayer rising to heaven. Fathers of the Church such as St John Chrysostom saw the evening incense as a penitential rite of self-offering to God. Traditionally it has been used to incense altar and people – two of the presences of Christ.

Incense is burned during the gospel canticle. People may be invited to put incense on the charcoal if it is used in the Introduction and during the intercessions. There are various ways of burning incense: the simplest method is to place the burning charcoal in a specially prepared heat-proof bowl, and place the incense in a container beside it; or a thurible could be used.

Other Symbols

Other visual elements might include:
- an **icon** representing Christ or the particular feast,
- **water** during the season of Easter as a reminder of our baptism.

Attention should also be given to **plants** or other **decor** which could enhance the environment and provide a seasonal accompaniment for the rite.

The traditional way of celebrating feasts and seasons has been through the use of different colours. This, together with other aids and the sensitive use of space, should help express the different mood and message of each season: the bareness of Lent contrasted with the richness of Easter.

It is important to have a sense of balance not to overcrowd the celebration with too much nor to use inappropriate objects. A rule to follow is the advice of the Church to remain authentic and simple.

Ministry

All ministries are ministries of service, enabling the prayer of the community. In all liturgy, it is better that ministries be shared among several people rather than one person act as both reader and cantor, for example.

Presider

A priest or deacon exercises the ministerial role of presider. Where there is a need this form of liturgy may also be led by an appropriately-skilled lay minister. The ministry of presider requires:

- a sense of prayer,
- a presence through word, gesture and silence,
- a grasp of the liturgy itself, an idea of how the various parts fit together,
- an ability to enable others in their ministries,
- a perceptible competence in leading liturgical celebration.

A good presider is the leader of the assembly, able to open and conclude prayer, proclaim in word and song, lead when needed, follow when necessary. In Evening Prayer there is no obligation to give presiders a special chair or to set them apart. As first among equals they need to be part of the assembly yet also seen and heard by all. In some communities the various roles may be shared.

Musicians

Music is integral to liturgy. The human voice has always been the primary instrument of worship and the principal minister of music is the assembly. A **cantor** can lead the assembly, sing alone as required and also teach new settings. A second cantor or musician may seem a luxury but they can provide a lead for the assembly and a contrast and help to the cantor. An **organist** or **instrumentalist** helps sustain the singing and through music can create atmosphere and allow reflection.

Reader

He or she will be sensitive to the style and content of the scripture, aware of the importance of good diction and have a simple manner of delivery. The Intercessions could be announced by a second reader. Depending on circumstances the reader proclaims from a lectern, the ambo or reads from their place.

Other Ministries

- Preparing and clearing the worship space: moving furniture, lighting the candle(s), preparing the incense bowl;
- welcoming people and handing out what is necessary (leaflet, hymnbook, candle etc.);
- assisting the presider, carrying the candle in procession.

> There is a special and very close bond between Christ and those whom he makes members of his Body, the Church, through the sacrament of rebirth. Thus, from the Head all the riches belonging to the Son flow throughout the whole Body: the communication of the Spirit, the truth, the life, and the participation in the divine sonship that Christ manifested in all his prayer when dwelt among us...
>
> The excellence of Christian prayer lies in its sharing in the reverent love of the only-begotten Son for the Father and in the prayers that the Son put into words in his earthly life and that still continues without ceasing in the name of the whole human race and for its salvation, throughout the universal Church and all its members.
>
> GILH 7

Elements of Evening Prayer

Structure

Evening prayer consists of four sections: **Introduction, Psalmody, Word, Prayer**. Each section has a number of parts. Evening Prayer begins with the **Introduction**: a hymn, opening responses, a liturgical action involving either light or incense. The section is concluded by the Opening Prayer.

Psalms are integral to the liturgy of the hours; in this version there is a seasonal psalm and a New Testament Canticle.

The scripture reading, the response and the Magnificat, the **Word** section, emphasise the reflective character of this liturgy.

Prayer has always been an essential part of the worship of the Christian community; prayer for the church, the community and the world.

There follows a more detailed description of the components of liturgical prayer.

Repetition

The material in this book is intended to be repeated over a series of weeks so that not only the structure of the prayer will become familiar to people but also the texts themselves. There are suggestions that some texts are changed with the liturgical seasons; other settings, such as the Magnificat, might not be changed for a longer period to allow people to get to know and pray the texts. Though this form of prayer may initially be new to many people in the beginning it is desired that through repetition of common elements it will provide a welcome opportunity for prayer and praise to God. Planners and musicians need to respect this aspect of the prayer rather than be continually seeking after novelty.

Prayer

In the liturgy prayer is greater than the spoken texts prayed by the presider and the assembly. Prayer is the shared silent response to a passage of scripture, the graceful lighting of a candle or placing of some incense on an incense burner.

Silence

Every liturgy needs moments of silence so that people can reflect on what they have heard and listen to the voice of God speaking to them. Silence helps to give a celebration pace and flow leading from one element to another. Different groups will have different capacities for silence and those leading the prayer need to be sensitive to those who have gathered to pray together.

Posture

It is customary at Evening Prayer to stand for the Introduction, sit for the Psalmody and the Scripture readings, to stand for the Gospel Canticle – the Magnificat – and remain standing until the conclusion of the prayer.

Music

Many of the texts of Evening Prayer are intended to be sung: the hymn, the psalm and canticle and the Magnificat. Music brings another dimension to the celebration. It allows all to sing with one voice and it can help give expression to the text. Communities should choose carefully what it is sung according to what is available and to their resources. Through repetition it is hoped that people will become familiar with settings.

Word

Scripture is integral to the prayer of the Church. It is the source of the psalms and canticles; it is the inspiration for hymns and prayers. The scripture reading is a time for reflection within Evening Prayer and all should be done to aid people's reflection. It should normally be read from the ambo by someone who is commissioned as a reader. The reading should be read from a worthy book: a lectionary or bible or a folder that has been prepared for the readings.

Dismissal

At the end of the celebration all are dismissed to live out the prayer in their daily lives. Some gatherings may wish to end with an informal sign of peace as a way of concluding the liturgy. In the material in Appendix 3 it notes that there may be occasions in the year when it may be appropriate to end the celebration with refreshments.

Preparing Evening Prayer

How the remainder of this book is organised.

Rather than give a number of fixed liturgies for the liturgical year it is hoped that the flexible arrangement of the structure together with the resources allow for liturgies to be prepared according to the needs of a community.

The resources are laid out following the structure of Evening Prayer. There is a detailed descriptions of each part, texts and appropriate music. Also included are the 'Assembly editions' which may be used in participation aids.

The book is completed by a number of appendices. Appendix 3 offers two complete model liturgies together with model participation aids. Also included here is a description of how this material might be used in a typical parish.

This section is to help communities prepare to celebrate Evening Prayer. Though the material in this book is intended for the weekly celebration of Evening Prayer, it can easily be used for individual seasons and celebrations.

This chapter is divided into three sections:

1 **Preparing** – what needs to be done in preparation;
2 **Celebrating** – an overview of the structure of Evening Prayer;
3 **Adapting** – what can be adapted for various occasions and what is provided.

1 Preparing Evening Prayer

A Preparation Group

Before beginning to celebrate Evening Prayer it may be helpful to establish a preparation group. They could be drawn from a parish liturgy committee, another parish group or be newly established. The task of the group will be to prepare the liturgies and help prepare the assembly for celebration. This section raises many of the issues the group will need to consider.

The group should aim to plan a season at a time. At the next meeting reflect on the liturgies you have previously celebrated before planning the next season.

A preparation leaflet is provided in Appendix 1, page 144.

When to start?
A central aspect of the liturgies in this book is that through repetition of structure, text and music our participation in the prayer is deepened.

It would be ideal to start with one of the liturgical seasons of Advent or Lent when people look to the Church to provide opportunities for communal prayer. The length and themes of the season also give the liturgies a clear framework.

Who celebrates?
The whole parish community should be invited to participate in Evening Prayer. It is important to remember that though only a few people may attend they pray as the parish community and as part of the universal Church.

People need to be informed, through newsletters, announcements, posters and personal invitation, that Evening Prayer will be celebrated.

Liturgical Space
Where is the most appropriate space in your church?
- *See* Gathering *on page 12.*

Symbol
What symbols will be used? Light, Incense?

Will the liturgical season be expressed in the environment?
- *See* Symbol *on page 13.*

Ministry
Identify the following ministers: Presider, Musician (Cantor, Accompanist), Reader.

What other ministries will you need?
- *See* Ministry *on page 14.*

Music

Repeat the musical settings of some parts such as the Magnificat or the New Testament Canticle from season to season allowing other parts which change with the season to be learnt with ease.

For parishes with few musical resources start with just singing the hymn and a metrical version of the Magnificat. Omit the Light and Incense service and the New Testament Canticle. (See notes in Appendix 3.)

Participation Aids

Many parishes already provide leaflets for Sunday Mass or special occasions. The purpose of this book is to provide a structure that local communities can adapt using material they are familiar with. Rather than providing a people's booklet which might make choices that are better made locally, this book provides the resources for communities to prepare their own leaflets. One of the principles is that material is repeated from week to week so one leaflet can be used over a season. As examples, two model leaflets are provided in Appendix 3. Appendix 4 gives details of the available resources. For information about the use of Assembly Editions see the Acknowledgements section (page 186).

Though leaflets will be necessary for people's participation, the preparation group will need to consider how else their participation can be enabled.

2 Celebrating Evening Prayer

Structure

The structure used in this book for Evening Prayer is outlined overleaf. In the following section there is a note of any choices that have to be made and a summary of any comments found in the resource section.

Introduction

Hymn/Opening Responses   33

There is a choice whether to start with a hymn or the Opening Responses. The *Divine Office* begins with the Responses but the Hymn could accompany an Entrance Procession, for example.

If the Light or Incense service follows it may be best to begin with the hymn so that there is a space between the musical items.

Hymn   33

Criteria for choosing hymns together with suggestions are provided.

Opening Responses   36

Two texts are provided. The first, with seasonal variations, when there is a light service. An informal welcome may follow.

Opening Rite: Light – Incense – Thanksgiving   37

One of these elements is chosen. In the section on adaptation below a suggestion is made for each season. For more solemn celebrations the Light or Incense may be followed by a Thanksgiving (which replaces the prayer).

Light   38

Candles are lit from a central candle during the singing of a response (with optional psalm verses). The section concludes with a prayer.

Incense   42

Incense is placed on burning charcoal during the singing of a response (with optional psalm verses). The section concludes with a prayer.

Thanksgiving   47

A Thanksgiving is provided for each season.

Introduction

Hymn	or	Opening Responses
─────		─────
Opening Responses		Hymn

Light	or	Incense	or	Thanks-giving
Collect		Collect		

Psalmody

Psalm

Psalm Prayer

New Testament Canticle

Word

Scripture Reading

Response

Magnificat

Prayer

Intercessions

Lord's Prayer

Concluding Prayer and Blessing

Psalmody

Psalm   54

You will need to decide how the psalm will be sung – ways of reciting the psalm are given on page 55. The psalm is followed by a period of silence and a psalm prayer.

In Ordinary Time some communities may find it preferable to use the four psalms provided for Ordinary Time as a four-week cycle – Week 1: Psalm 90, Week 2: Psalm 120, Week 3: Psalm 109, Week 4: Psalm 138.

A supplement of four psalms is provided for those who wish to enrich the celebration with a second psalm.

New Testament Canticle   95

You will need to decide how the canticle will be sung. One setting can be used throughout the year (except in Lent). If it is not sung it may be omitted.

Word

Scripture Reading   104

A reading will need to be chosen. It is presumed that the response to the reading will normally be silence but alternatives are provided.

Magnificat   107

Any of the settings can be used, and repeated, throughout the year.

Incense may be burned during the proclamation of the Magnificat.

Prayer

Intercessions   122

Communities can use those provided, take them from other sources or prepare their own.

Lord's Prayer   133

The Lord's Prayer may be followed by a sign of peace or this may be done at the end of the celebration.

Concluding Prayer and Blessing   138

A choice of texts is provided.

3 Adapting Evening Prayer

Progressive Solemnity

The *General Introduction to the Liturgy of the Hours* outlined the principle of 'progressive solemnity' (273) – the variety of stages between a said Office and a fully sung liturgy according to local resources and need (Appendix 3 shows how this might be explored in an ordinary parish). Care should be taken that through the year the celebrations of the Easter season, for example, are 'more solemn' than those for Ordinary Time.

Liturgical Seasons

The year is divided into eight seasons:

Advent	
Christmas	
Ordinary Time 1	*between the Christmas Season and the beginning of Lent*
Lent	
Easter	
Ordinary Time 2	*from the end of the Easter Season until the end of July*
Ordinary Time 3	*August–September*
Ordinary Time 4	*October–November (until the beginning of Advent)*

Some material, such as psalms, is seasonal and is listed below; for other parts there are seasonal suggestions.

Advent

Seasonal Resources:

- Opening Response A
- Light Service (*recommended*)
- Thanksgiving
- Psalm 84
- Intercessions
- Lord's Prayer Introduction
- Concluding Prayer

Advent Wreath

The *Book of Blessings* suggests that the blessing of the Advent Wreath and lighting of its first candle takes place during the first Evening Prayer of the first Sunday of Advent on Saturday evening. Material for the intercessions and blessing is available in the *Book of Blessings*.

Christmas
Seasonal Resources:
- Opening Response A
- Light Service (*recommended*)
- Thanksgiving
- Psalm 23
- Intercessions
- Lord's Prayer Introduction
- Concluding Prayer

Ordinary Time I
between the Christmas Season and the beginning of Lent
Seasonal Resources:
- Light Service (*recommended*)
- Psalm 90
- Intercessions
- Thanksgiving (*general choice for Ordinary Time*)
- Concluding Prayer (*general choice for Ordinary Time*)

Week of Prayer for Christian Unity
The liturgy of the hours is a format shared by many of the churches and so is well suited to an ecumenical celebration. To aid participation choose a hymn that is familiar to all. The use of Taizé chant for the Response is also appropriate. It may be appropriate to emphasise the 'Catholic' elements – candles and incense.

Lent
Seasonal Resources:
- Incense Service (*recommended*)
- Thanksgiving
- Psalm 129
- Intercessions
- Lord's Prayer Introduction
- Concluding Prayer

Easter
Seasonal Resources:
- Opening Response A
- Light Service (*recommended*)
- Thanksgiving
- Psalm 113a
- Intercessions
- Lord's Prayer Introduction
- Concluding Prayer

Easter Sunday
The Triduum ends with Evening Prayer on Easter Sunday. This is an opportunity for reflection on the events of the previous night. During the liturgy all process to the baptismal font and are blessed with water (see model liturgy Appendix 3).

Pentecost
Traditionally the Paschal Candle is processed to the font at the end of Evening Prayer.

Ordinary Time II
from the end of the Easter Season until the end of July
Seasonal Resources:
- Incense Service (*recommended*)
- Psalm 120
- Intercessions
- Thanksgiving (*general choice for Ordinary Time*)
- Concluding Prayer (*general choice for Ordinary Time*)

Ordinary Time III
August – September
Seasonal Resources:
- Incense Service (*recommended*)
- Psalm 109
- Intercessions
- Thanksgiving (*general choice for Ordinary Time*)
- Concluding Prayer (*general choice for Ordinary Time*)

Ordinary Time IV
October – November (until the beginning of Advent)
Seasonal Resources:
- Incense Service (*recommended*)
- Psalm 138
- Intercessions
- Thanksgiving (*general choice for Ordinary Time*)
- Concluding Prayer (*general choice for Ordinary Time*)

Adapting through the year

Solemnities and Feasts of the Lord
When a Solemnity (e.g., St Peter and St Paul) or a Feast of the Lord (e.g., Triumph of the Cross) displaces the Sunday of Ordinary Time this should be marked in the celebration of Evening Prayer by the choice of an appropriate hymn and the use of the Concluding Prayer from the *Divine Office*. For a list of celebrations that can fall on a Sunday see Appendix 2.

Anniversary of Dedication
The anniversary of a church's dedication is celebrated as a Solemnity in the dedicated church. It can be marked by a celebration of Evening Prayer. This might include both Light (including the lighting of the dedication candles) and Incense to recall their significance in the Rite of Dedication. An appropriate hymn can be chosen together with a Concluding Prayer from the *Divine Office*.

Cycle of Prayer
Evening Prayer is an appropriate way to celebrate the themes of the Cycle of Prayer (Appendix 2). The choice of hymn, psalm or reading could be adapted. The theme should be included in the Intercessions. A second non-biblical reading might be added after the response.

Weekdays
The liturgies in this book can be simplified for use during the week. It is important to differentiate between a Sunday and a weekday celebration in how the liturgy is celebrated. To do this it is possible to omit one or more of the following elements: Light–Incense–Thanksgiving, Magnificat, New Testament Canticle.

A short form for meetings

A shortened form of Evening Prayer is suitable for the beginning or end of a parish meeting. Using material from this book, the following structure would reflect the earliest forms of Evening Prayer.

Opening Responses
Psalm
Intercessions
Lord's Prayer

Funerals

The *Order of Christian Funerals* recommends Evening Prayer as a format for the Reception of the Body or as a Vigil. The Reception of the Body would replace the Opening Responses, the Hymn and Thanksgiving.

- Suitable psalms include 120 (page 76), 129 (page 68).
- There is an opportunity for a member of the family or a friend to speak some words of remembrance before the dismissal.
- Examples of prayers and intercessions are included in Part IV of the *Order of Christian Funerals*.

Eucharistic Exposition

The form of celebration would be as follows:

Exposition (Song, Exposition),
Evening Prayer,
Time of silent prayer,
[Benediction (Eucharistic Song, Prayer, Blessing)]
and Reposition (Reposition, Acclamation)

[Benediction – optional when a priest or deacon presides.]

Reference should be made to *Holy Communion and Worship of the Eucharist outside Mass* for texts and more detail.

Mass
The *General Instruction on the Liturgy of the Hours* (93, 96, 94) gives the following outline in those special cases where Evening Prayer is joined with Mass:

Hymn
Greeting
Psalmody
[Gloria]
Opening Prayer of Mass
Liturgy of the Word
Intercessions
Liturgy of the Eucharist
Communion
Magnificat
Post Communion Prayer
Concluding Rite

Evening Prayer and Communion

This form of Evening Prayer will only be celebrated where allowed for by diocesan norms. Communion would be distributed at a celebration of Evening Prayer only where Mass has not taken place that day and there is no priest available:

Introduction
Psalmody
Word
    Intercessions
Communion
    Magnificat
    Concluding Prayer and Blessing

On Sundays where this is the community's only liturgy it would be appropriate to include the whole of the Liturgy of the Word.

RESOURCES

LET
MY
PRAYER
ARISE
BEFORE
YOULIKE

INCENSE

Introduction

Structure

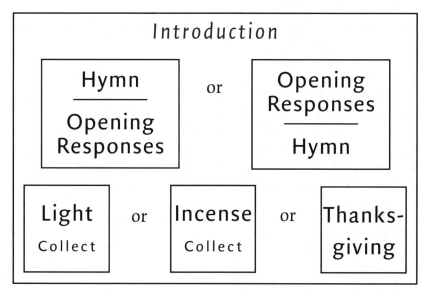

Hymn

From the earliest times hymns have been sung at Evening Prayer.

Text

When choosing a hymn ensure that all the verses are appropriate for evening prayer and reflect one or more of the following themes:

- light/evening – the time of day, the lighting of lamps, Christ the light of the world; avoid hymns that are about morning or night-time.
- season/feast – the liturgical season, such as Lent, or the day itself.
- thanksgiving – for the day that has been, for Christ's work of redemption.

Other themes are less appropriate for Evening Prayer, e.g., eucharistic devotion, Marian (other than on feasts of Our Lady). Also to be avoided are paraphrases of psalms. Poetry is more suitable for personal recitation.

Use

When a hymn begins the celebration it accompanies any procession of ministers. However, the procession may be in silence and the liturgy begin with the responses.

Where there is no Light Service any candles will be already lit before the beginning of the liturgy.

Hymns

The following list is not meant in any way to be exhaustive. It highlights seasonal hymns that speak of the evening or light, for example. For each season there will be many other hymns. Those celebrating Evening Prayer over the Christmas season will find that many carols are suitable; though ones that speak of 'Christmas morn' should be avoided. Titles of hymns may differ from book to book.

Advent

Come thou long expected Jesus
Creator of the stars of night
Litany of the Word
Lo, he comes
My soul in stillness waits §
O come, divine Messiah!
O come, O come Emmanuel §
O comfort my people
O Wisdom, source of harmony §
The Coming of our God
The Voice of God

   § These hymns, based on the 'O' Antiphons, are usually sung after
   17 December.

Christmas

Jesus the Word
Of the Father's love begotten
O little town of Bethlehem
The Light of Christ

Lent

Dear Lord and Father
Lord Jesus, as we turn from sin
Praise to the holiest in the height
Praise to you, O Christ our Saviour

Easter

Sing of one who walks beside us
The light of Christ
This joyful Eastertide
We walk by faith

Ordinary Time

Abide with me
As the setting sun
Christ, be our light
Christ is the world's light
God of day and God of darkness
In the quiet of the evening
Light of Gladness
Lord of all hopefulness
Now it is evening
Now the evening
O gladsome light
O Gracious Light
The day thou gavest

Other Resources include:

The Divine Office (HarperCollins)
Cantate (Decani Music)
Hymnal of the Hours (GIA publications)
Hymns for Prayer and Praise (Canterbury Press)
    prepared by The Panel of Monastic Musicians

Opening Responses

The choice of opening response is determined by the following rite: if light is the focus, A is used; otherwise B is used.

- The order of the hymn and the response can be reversed.
- The responses may be followed, if necessary, by a short informal welcome.

A

Presider	Jesus Christ, you are the light of the world:
All	**the light no darkness can overcome;**
Presider	Stay with us now, for it is evening,
All	**and the day is almost over.**
Presider	Let your light scatter the darkness,
All	**and shine among your people here.**

The first line can be varied according to the season.

Advent	Jesus Christ, promised Messiah, you are the light of the world:
Christmas	Jesus Christ, Word made flesh, you are the light of the world:
Lent	Jesus Christ, Saviour of all, you are the light of the world:
Easter	Jesus Christ, risen in glory, you are the light of the world:

B

Presider	O God, come to our aid.
All	**O Lord, make haste to help us.**
Presider	Glory be to the Father, and to the Son and to the Holy Spirit,
All	**as it was in the beginning,**
	is now and ever shall be world without end. Amen.
	Alleluia. *(except in Lent)*

Opening Rite
Light – Incense – Thanksgiving

In this section of the Introduction there is a choice between a Light or Incense Service and a Thanksgiving. It is suggested that the focus should be **light** during the following seasons: Advent, Christmas, Ordinary Time 1 (Winter), Easter, Ordinary Time 4 (Autumn); **incense** during Lent and Ordinary Time 2 and 3 – during the Summer when Evening Prayer will be celebrated by most communities before sunset. Communities may wish to change this pattern; it is recommended that whichever focus is chosen it is kept for the season. Communities wishing to develop their celebration of Evening Prayer may wish to celebrate with two of the elements: Light and Thanksgiving or Incense and Thanksgiving. For solemn celebrations all three elements could be used. Where there are few musical resources the actions of light and incense could be carried out in silence. The Opening Rite may also be omitted.

LIGHT

A candle is placed centrally and lit before the beginning of the liturgy.
The light reminds us of Christ the light of the world and the approaching
night. During the singing of the chant and verses other candles are lit by
members of the assembly. The section is concluded by a prayer.

Either of the following chants is sung as an ostinato, or with selected verses

Send out your light

Send out your light, Lord, send your truth to be my guide.

Then let them lead me to the place where you reside.

text and music: John L Bell

The Lord is my light

Theme I

The Lord is my light, my light and sal-va-tion: in

him I trust, in him I trust. The

Theme II

The Lord is my light, my light and sal-va-tion: in

him I trust, in him I trust. The

Accompaniment

The Lord is my light may be sung as a 4-part canon or Theme I and II
may be sung together or any combination of these together.

music: Taizé – Jacques Berthier

Optional Verses

The following verses are taken from the psalms. As many verses as necessary are selected to accompany the liturgical action. Further verses may be added if required.

O come, bless the Lord,
   all you who <u>serve</u> the Lord
who stand watch in the house of the Lord
   in the courts of the house <u>of</u> our God.   *133 (134)*

The Lord is my light and my help
   whom <u>should</u> I fear?
The Lord is the stronghold of my life;
   before whom <u>shall</u> I shrink?   *26 (27)*

I have called to you, Lord, hasten to help me!
   Hear my voice when I <u>cry</u> to you.
Let my prayer arise before you like incense,
   my hands uplifted like the <u>eve</u>ning sacrifice.   *140 (141)*

A pure heart create for me, O God,
   put a steadfast sp<u>irit</u> within me.
My sacrifice, a contrite spirit.
   A humbled, contrite heart you <u>will</u> not spurn.
                                    50 (51):12, 19

In you, O Lord, I take refuge,
   let me never be <u>put</u> to shame.
Into your hands I commend my spirit;
   it is you who will re<u>deem</u> me, Lord.   *30 (31):2, 6*

O praise the Lord, all you nations,
   acclaim him, <u>all</u> you peoples!
Strong is his love for us;
   he is faith<u>ful</u> for ever!   *116 (117)*

The section concludes with one of the following prayers. If Light is followed by the Thanksgiving (page 47) the prayer may be omitted.

Presider   Let us pray.

Pause for silent prayer.

A   Yours is the day and yours the night, Lord God:
              let the Sun of Justice shine so steadily in our hearts,
              that we may come at length
              to that light where you dwell eternally.
              We ask this through our Lord Jesus Christ, your Son,
              who lives and reigns with you in the unity of the Holy Spirit,
              God for ever and ever.

All   **Amen.**

or B   Lord God,
              it is our bounden duty to proclaim you as the Light
              with whom there is no alteration or shadow of change:
              enlighten our darkness as we reach the close of this day,
              and in your mercy forgive us our sins.
              We ask this through our Lord Jesus Christ, your Son,
              who lives and reigns with you in the unity of the Holy Spirit,
              God for ever and ever.

All   **Amen.**

or C   Stay with us, Lord Jesus, as evening falls:
              be our companion on our way.
              In your mercy inflame our hearts and raise our hope,
              so that, in union with your Church,
              we may recognise you in the scriptures,
              and in the breaking of Bread.
              Who lives and reign with the Father and the Holy Spirit,
              God, for ever and ever.

All   **Amen.**

Other resources

Come, light of the world	Foster	C
Jesus Christ, yesterday,	Toolan	L, G
Kindle a flame	Iona	EOA
Lumen Christi	Lécot	LHON
Our darkness	Taizé	C

INCENSE

An incense burner is placed centrally with burning charcoals before the liturgy. The burning of incense has long been a sign of penitence and an image of our prayer rising to God. During the chant members of the assembly may place grains of incense on the charcoal. It is concluded by a prayer.

Either of the following chants is sung as an ostinato, or with selected verses.

Let my prayer

Optional Verses

1	𝄽	Lord, _____	hear	my	voice when I	call; __
2	Your	love and your	faith -	ful - ness	are with	me. __
3	Here___	in your	ho -	ly	place I	re - vere you;
4	𝄽	Lord, _____	set	a	guard on my	mouth._
5	𝄽	𝄽	I will bow___	down__	be - fore	you.

O	hear_____	me	when I	call.
I	praise	your	ho - - - ly	name.
I	give _____	thanks	for your	name.
O	turn	my	heart____	from wrong.
In	you	my	soul is	at peace.

The verses, from Psalm 140 (141), are sung over the harmonies of the refrain (which can be sung to 'Ah' underneath).

text and music: Christopher Walker

O Lord, hear my prayer

music: Taizé — Jacques Berthier

Optional Verses

The following verses are taken from the psalms. As many verses as necessary are selected to accompany the liturgical action. Further verses may be added if necessary. If it is desired to use the verses with Let my prayer the tone in D minor (page 40) should be used.

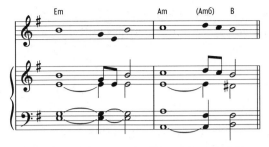

O come, bless the Lord,
  all you who <u>serve</u> the Lord
who stand watch in the house of the Lord
  in the courts of the house <u>of</u> our God. *133 (134)*

The Lord is my light and my help
  whom <u>should</u> I fear?
The Lord is the stronghold of my life;
  before whom <u>shall</u> I shrink? *26 (27)*

I have called to you, Lord, hasten to help me!
  Hear my voice when I <u>cry</u> to you.
Let my prayer arise before you like incense,
  my hands uplifted like the <u>eve</u>ning sacrifice. *140 (141)*

A pure heart create for me, O God,
  put a steadfast sp<u>ir</u>it within me.
My sacrifice, a contrite spirit.
  A humbled, contrite heart you <u>will</u> not spurn.
                                          50 (51):12, 19

In you, O Lord, I take refuge,
  let me never be <u>put</u> to shame.
Into your hands I commend my spirit;
  it is you who will re<u>deem</u> me, Lord. *30 (31):2, 6*

O praise the Lord, all you nations,
  acclaim him, <u>all</u> you peoples!
Strong is his love for us;
  he is fai<u>thful</u> for ever! *116 (117)*

The section concludes with one of the following prayers. If Incense is followed by the Thanksgiving (page 47) the prayer may be omitted.

Presider   Let us pray.

Pause for silent prayer.

A   We give you thanks, Lord God Almighty,
     for bringing us safely to the evening of this day;
     we humbly ask that the prayer we make with uplifted hands
     may be an offering pleasing in your sight.
     We ask this through our Lord Jesus Christ, your Son,
     who lives and reigns with you in the unity of the Holy Spirit,
     God for ever and ever.

All   **Amen.**

or B   All powerful God,
     since you have given us, your unworthy servants,
     the strength to work throughout this day:
     accept this evening sacrifice of praise
     as we thank you for your gifts.
     We ask this through our Lord Jesus Christ, your Son,
     who lives and reigns with you in the unity of the Holy Spirit,
     God for ever and ever.

All   **Amen.**

or C   Let our evening prayer rise up before your throne of mercy, Lord,
     and let your blessing come down upon us:
     so that now and for ever
     your grace may help and save us.
     We ask this through our Lord Jesus Christ, your Son,
     who lives and reigns with you in the unity of the Holy Spirit,
     God for ever and ever.

All   **Amen.**

Other resources

Ps 140 (141)	Dean	L
Ps 140 (141)	Haugen	G
Ps 140 (141)	Inwood	CTSF
Ps 140 (141)	Joncas	L
Ps 140 (141)	Russian, arr. Dean	C
Incense rites	Griffiths	*Celebrating the Christian Year*

THANKSGIVING

For communities with few musical resources the thanksgiving can be the best option.

A candle is placed centrally and lit before the beginning of the liturgy. The thanksgiving is said by the presider. The prayer expresses one or more of these themes: thanksgiving for Christ and our redemption in him, thanksgiving for the day which is ending, thanksgiving for the light in our midst.

Advent

Presider	Let us give thanks to the Lord our God.
All	**It is right to give him thanks and praise.**
Presider	Blessed are you, Sovereign God, creator of light and darkness! As evening falls, you renew your promise to reveal among us the light of your presence. May your word be a lantern to our feet and a light upon our path, that we may behold your glory coming among us. Strengthen us in our stumbling weakness and free our tongues to sing your praise, Father, Son and Holy Spirit:
All	**Blessed be God forever!**

Christmas

Presider	Let us give thanks to the Lord our God
All	**It is right to give him thanks and praise.**
Presider	Blessed are you, Sovereign God, our light and our salvation, to you be glory and praise for ever! In the beginning you laid the foundation of the earth, and the heavens are the work of your hands. To dispel the darkness of our night, you sent forth your Son, the first–born of all creation. He is our Christ, the light of the world, and him we acclaim, as all creation sings to you, Father, Son and Holy Spirit:
All	**Blessed be God for ever!**

Lent

Presider Let us give thanks to the Lord our God
All **It is right to give him thanks and praise.**
Presider Blessed are you, Sovereign God,
Shepherd of your pilgrim people:
pillar of cloud by day,
pillar of fire by night.
In these forty days you lead us
in prayer, fasting, and reflection,
that we may find grace in the wilderness,
and attain the freedom of your new creation.
Stir up in us the fire of your love
which shone forth from your Son
enthroned on the cross,
that, cleansed from all our sin,
we may be made ready to come into your presence,
Father, Son, and Holy Spirit:
All **Blessed be God for ever!**

Easter

Presider Let us give thanks to the Lord our God
All **It is right to give him thanks and praise.**
Presider Blessed are you, Sovereign God,
our light and our salvation;
to you be glory and praise for ever!
You led your people to freedom
by a pillar of cloud by day
and a pillar of fire by night,
May we who walk in the light of your presence
acclaim your Christ, rising victorious,
as he banishes all darkness from our hearts and minds,
and praise you, Father, Son and Holy Spirit:
All **Blessed be God for ever!**

Ordinary Time

Four texts for the Thanksgiving are given for Ordinary Time. They can be used according to the section of Ordinary Time (1, 2...), as a four-week cycle or ad libitum.

Ordinary Time A

Presider   Let us give thanks to the Lord our God

All   **It is right to give him thanks and praise.**

Presider   We praise and thank you, O God,
for you are without beginning or end.
Through Christ, you created the whole world;
in Christ, you preserve it.
You are God and Father,
the giver of the Spirit,
the ruler of all that is seen and unseen.
You made the day for works of light
and night for refreshment of our minds and bodies.
O loving Lord and source of all that is good,
graciously accept our evening sacrifice of praise,
for you are worthy of all honour and glory,
Father, Son and Holy Spirit:

All   **Blessed be God for ever!**

Ordinary Time B

Presider   Let us give thanks to the Lord our God

All   **It is right to give him thanks and praise.**

Presider   Blessed are you, O Lord Redeemer God.
You destroyed the bonds of death
and from the darkness of the tomb
drew forth the Light of the world.
Through Christ we have become children of the light
reborn in baptism and sealed by the Spirit.
With all creation we sing your praise,
Father, Son and Holy Spirit:

All   **Blessed be God for ever!**

Ordinary Time C

Presider Let us give thanks to the Lord our God

All **It is right to give him thanks and praise.**

Presider Blessed are you,
Lord God of all creation;
through your goodness
we kindle the light of evening
which you have given
to dispel the coming darkness.
Let it be for us
a witness to your undying light
Father, Son and Holy Spirit.

All **Blessed be God for ever.**

Ordinary Time D

Presider Let us give thanks to the Lord our God

All **It is right to give him thanks and praise.**

Presider We give you thanks, O God,
through your Son Jesus Christ;
because you have shone out for us
as a light that never fades.
You have given us the daylight
to gladden the heart,
and now in your compassion
you offer us the light of evening
to dispel the darkness of the coming night.
For this we praise you
and give you glory
through Jesus Christ
In the Holy Spirit
now and always
for ever and ever:

All **Amen.**

Resources

Further examples of Thanksgivings may be found in:
Celebrating Common Prayer (Mowbray)
Praise God in Song (GIA Publications): *includes musical settings.*

Assembly editions

For information about the use of Assembly Editions see the Acknowledgements section (page 186).

Light

Send out your light, Lord, send your truth to be my guide.

Then let them lead me to the place where you re-side.

The Lord is my light, my light and sal-va-tion: in

him I trust, in him I trust. The

Incense

Let my prayer rise be-fore you like in-cense.

Let my prayer come to you, my God.

Let my

O Lord, hear my prayer, O Lord, hear my prayer;

when I call an-swer me. O Lord, hear my prayer, O

Lord, hear my prayer. Come and lis-ten to me. O

Psalmody

Structure

Psalmody

Psalm

Psalm Prayer

New Testament Canticle

Psalm

The psalms are the kernel of the Prayer of the Church linking us with the Hebrew tradition of daily worship. From the Gospels we learn that the psalms were constantly on the lips of Christ, in prayer and in teaching.

In praying the psalms today, we pray with and through him, we make his prayer our own. The psalms express the range of human emotions: praise, thanksgiving, sorrow, supplication, hope and despair, shared by all at different times.

It is worth remembering that the Prayer of the Church is universal. It is the prayer of the Body of Christ as the local community and as the whole Church: 'If one part of the Body suffers, all suffer; if one part rejoices, all rejoice' (1 Cor. 12:26). Through the psalms, and through the whole of evening prayer, we pray, not just for ourselves and our individual needs but for, and with, the whole Church.

The repetition of the psalms enables us to take to heart the words, so that their language becomes part of our language of prayer. This repetition also emphasises our continuing call to conversion as we listen to the voice of God in the psalms.

The season of Ordinary Time has been divided into four parts (see page 24): a psalm is given for each part. Some communities, however, may prefer to use the four psalms for Ordinary Time as a four-week cycle.

Four supplementary psalms are given following page 83. This offers a second psalm for those comunities that wish to enrich the celebration. The setting of Psalm 116 (page 84) can be used as a simple tone with an Alleluia response; it can be used as an alternative tone and response to any of the psalms.

Ways of Reciting the Psalm
Psalm Tone

The preferred method of reciting the psalms is using a psalm tone. This allows the liturgical text to be used and the simplicity of the tone allows the text to speak.

Two types of psalm tone are used. They are sometimes distinguished by names of composers associated with them: Laurence **Bévenot** and Joseph **Gelineau.**

Bévenot type tones ((B) *the letter is used to indicate the type of settings in the lists of 'Other settings'. A list of types is on page 58)* are used for the majority of the psalm in this resource. They consist of a four-bar tone which is used with four-line psalm verses. In longer verses lines are either run on or a portion of the tone is repeated. In shorter verses bars are omitted. The text should be sung with a light clear voice at a pace suitable for proclamation.

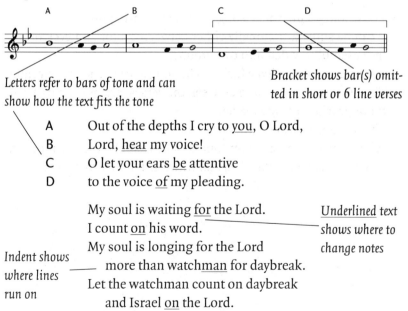

Letters refer to bars of tone and can show how the text fits the tone

Bracket shows bar(s) omitted in short or 6 line verses

A	Out of the depths I cry to <u>you</u>, O Lord,
B	Lord, <u>hear</u> my voice!
C	O let your ears <u>be</u> attentive
D	to the voice <u>of</u> my pleading.

My soul is waiting <u>for</u> the Lord.
I count <u>on</u> his word.
My soul is longing for the Lord
    more than watch<u>man</u> for daybreak.
Let the watchman count on daybreak
    and Israel <u>on</u> the Lord.

Indent shows where lines run on

Underlined text shows where to change notes

Gelineau tones (G) (cf. Ps 113a) are sung to a regular pulse. The note changes according to the accent of the text.

> When Israel came forth from Egypt,
> Jacob's sons from an alien people,
> Judah became the Lord's temple,
> Israel became God's kingdom.

is sung as follows:

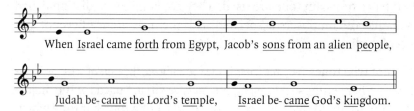

When Israel came forth from Egypt, Jacob's sons from an alien people,

Judah be- came the Lord's temple,   Israel be- came God's kingdom.

Performance

Each psalm is provided with a tone and an optional response. These can be used in the following ways:

- The whole psalm can be sung by everyone throughout.
- It can be sung antiphonally either between cantor and everyone or the assembly divided into two groups.
- A response is provided which can be sung at each end of the psalm.
- The response can be sung between the verses, either sung by a cantor or proclaimed by a reader.
- The response may be omitted.
- When introducing a psalm tone to an assembly it is often best to sing it to the text of the *Glory be...* which is familiar to people.

Alternative settings

After each psalm a list of other settings is given. It can include both further psalm tones and other types of psalm setting, such as lyrical settings and psalm paraphrases.

- Resources for the Responsorial Psalm at Sunday Mass may also provide familiar settings for some communities though, as noted below, they will often comprise of part of the psalm text.

Lyrical (Through Settings) (L)

These are more melodic setting of the psalms (e.g., *On Eagle's Wings*).

- The verses of these are often intended for solo cantor with a response sung by all.
- There are also settings available for choirs with a response for the congregation.
- Many such settings were originally written as a responsorial psalm for the Liturgy of the Word and will offer only a selection of verses.

Ostinato (O)

These are often Taizé chants.

- Verses from the psalm are sung by a cantor over a repeated phrase of music which is sung by all (the ostinato).
- The ostinato could also be played by an accompaniment while the verses are sung.
- The verses of the psalm could be read over the ostinato.

Psalm Paraphrase (Hymn) (P)

- Metrical settings of the psalms have a long tradition within Christian music. They are a good way to introduce the singing of psalms when psalm-tones appear too forbidding. However, the advantage of a tone is that it gives priority to the text.
- Introduce variety into how the paraphrase is sung, singing it antiphonally etc.

Reading the Psalm

- As stated in the *General Instruction* some psalms may be better said. (GILH 279)
- As with singing there is a variety of ways of reciting the psalms:
  - there can be a musical background to the reading or the response can be sung (not said) between verses.
  - psalms are best read by individual voices reflecting the structure where appropriate.
  - the psalms are first of all poetry and should be read as such.
  - communities are encouraged to sing the psalms.

Psalm Prayers

At the end of each psalm is a psalm prayer – a short collect said after the psalm by the presider.

> *Psalm prayers help those reciting the psalms to interpret them in a Christian way ... when the psalm is completed and a short silence is observed, the psalm prayer sums up the aspirations and emotions of those saying them.*
>
> GILH 112

Psalm descriptions – see page 55

B	Bévenot type
G	Gelineau type
L	Lyrical setting
O	Ostinato (Taizé)
P	Paraphrase
R	Response

Advent

Psalm 84 (85)

A	O Lord, you once fa<u>vou</u>red your land
B	and revived the for<u>tune</u>s of Jacob,
C	you forgave the guilt <u>of</u> your people
D	and covered <u>all</u> their sins.
A	You averted <u>all</u> your rage,
D	you calmed the heat <u>of</u> your anger.

Revive us now, <u>God</u>, our helper!
Put an end to your grie<u>van</u>ce against us.
Will you be angry with <u>us</u> for ever,
will your anger <u>never</u> cease?

Will you not restore ag<u>ain</u> our life
that your people may rej<u>oice</u> in you?
Let us see, O <u>Lord</u>, your mercy
and give us your <u>saving</u> help.

A	I will hear what the Lord <u>has</u> to say,
B	a voice that <u>speaks</u> of peace,
C	peace for his people <u>and</u> his friends
D	and those who turn to him <u>in</u> their hearts.
A	His help is near for <u>those</u> who fear him
D	and his glory will dwell <u>in</u> our land.

Mercy and faithful<u>ness</u> have met;
justice and peace <u>have</u> embraced.
Faithfulness shall spring <u>from</u> the earth
and justice look <u>down</u> from heaven.

The Lord will <u>make</u> us prosper
and our earth shall <u>yield</u> its fruit.
Justice shall <u>march</u> before him
and peace shall fol<u>low</u> his steps.

Glory be to the Father and <u>to</u> the Son
and to the <u>Ho</u>ly Spirit.
As it was in the beginning, is now,
    and <u>ev</u>er shall be,
world without <u>end</u>. Amen

The Lord will come from his ho - ly place;
he will come to save his peo - ple.

tone: *Laurence Bévenot* OSB

Presider	Revive us now, God our helper!
	restore us to fullness of life in you;
	that mercy and truth may be our guide
	and peace be a pathway for our feet.
	We ask this through Jesus Christ our Lord.
All	**Amen.**

Other settings

Let us see	Dean	VE	L
Lord, let us see	Haugen	G	L
Let us see	Smith	PS1, L, VE	B
Dona Nobis Pacem	Taizé	TV2, SP	O
O Christe Domine Jesu	Taizé	TV2, CFE	O

List of abbreviations – see Appendix 4 on page 180.
List of psalm types – see page 58.

Assembly editions

The Lord will come from his holy place;
he will come to save his people.

Let
your
light
scatter
the darkness
and shine among
your people here

Christmas

Psalm 23 (24)

The Lord's is the earth <u>and</u> its fullness,
the world and <u>all</u> its peoples.
It is he who set it <u>on</u> the seas;
on the waters he <u>made</u> it firm.

Who shall climb the mountain <u>of</u> the Lord?
Who shall stand in his <u>holy</u> place?
The man with clean hands <u>and</u> pure heart,
who desires not <u>worth</u>less things.

He shall receive blessings <u>from</u> the Lord
and reward from the <u>God</u> who saves them.
Such are the <u>men</u> who seek him,
seek the face of the <u>God</u> of Jacob.

A   O gates, lift <u>high</u> your heads;
C   grow higher, <u>an</u>cient doors.
D   Let him enter, the <u>king</u> of glory!

A   Who is the <u>king</u> of glory?
C   The Lord, the <u>mighty</u>, the valiant,
D   the Lord, the <u>valiant</u> in war.

A   O gates, lift <u>high</u> your heads;
C   grow higher, <u>an</u>cient doors.
D   Let him enter, the <u>king</u> of glory!

A   Who is he, the <u>king</u> of glory?
C   He, the <u>Lord</u> of armies,
D   He is the <u>king</u> of glory.

Glory be to the Father and <u>to</u> the Son
and to the <u>Ho</u>ly Spirit.
As it was in the beginning, is now,
    and <u>ev</u>er shall be,
world without <u>end</u>. Amen

tone: Martin Foster; response: James Walsh

Presider	King of glory,
	to whom the earth and all its fullness belongs;
	grant us purity of heart in seeking your face
	and honest hands in all our labours,
	so that we may be found fit to stand before you
	and receive the blessing of your salvation.
	We ask this through Jesus Christ our Lord.
All	**Amen.**

Other settings

Stretch towards heaven	Boulton Smith	PS1	L
Let the Lord enter	Ollis	PS3	L
King of Glory	Tamblyn	HIG	L

Assembly editions

O - pen your gates, raise your heads on high! Grow ev - er
high - er, ev - er - last - ing doors! Let him en - ter,
let him come in! He is king of glo - ry!

Lent
Psalm 129 (130)

Out of the depths I cry to <u>you</u>, O Lord,
Lord, <u>hear</u> my voice!
O let your ears <u>be</u> attentive
to the voice <u>of</u> my pleading.

If you, O Lord should <u>mark</u> our guilt,
Lord, who <u>would</u> survive?
But with you is <u>found</u> forgiveness:
for this <u>we</u> revere you.

My soul is waiting <u>for</u> the Lord.
I count <u>on</u> his word.
My soul is longing for the Lord
    more than watch<u>man</u> for daybreak.
Let the watchmen count on daybreak
    and Israel <u>on</u> the Lord.

Because with the Lord <u>there</u> is mercy
and fullness <u>of</u> redemption,
Israel indeed he <u>will</u> redeem
from all <u>its</u> iniquity.

Glory be to the Father and <u>to</u> the Son
and to the <u>Ho</u>ly Spirit.
As it was in the beginning, is now,
    and <u>ev</u>er shall be,
world without <u>end</u>. Amen

Presider	Be attentive to our voice, O Lord,
	and hear the longings of our heart;
	mark not our guilt
	but in your faithful love
	restore us to the fullness of redemption.
	We ask this through Jesus Christ our Lord.
All	**Amen.**

With the Lord there is mer-cy and full-ness of re-demp-tion.

tone: Laurence Bévenot OSB

Other settings

Out of direst depths	Bell	L, PPP	P
Out of the depths	Dean	C	R
Out of the depths	Gelineau	L	G
With the Lord	Haugen	G	L
From the depths of sin	Jabusch	CFE	P
Out of the depths	O'Hara	AK	L
From the depths	Smith	PS2	L
Out of the depths	Soper	L	L
Out of the depths	Walker	C	R
De profundis blues	Wellicome	PS3	L

Assembly editions

With the Lord there is mer-cy and full-ness of re-demp-tion.

Easter

Psalm 113a (114)

When Israel came forth from Egypt,
Jacob's sons from an alien people,
Judah became the Lord's temple,
Israel became God's kingdom.

The sea fled at the sight,
the Jordan turned back on its course,
the mountains leapt like rams
and the hills like yearling sheep.

Why was it sea, that you fled,
that you turned back, Jordan on your course?
Mountains that you leapt like rams;
hills, like yearling sheep?

Tremble, O earth, before the Lord,
in the presence of the God of Jacob,
who turns rock into a pool
and flint into a spring of water.

Give praise to the Father Almighty,
to his Son, Jesus Christ, the Lord,
to the Spirit who dwells in our hearts,
both now and for ever. Amen.

Presider   As if rivers should run backwards
or the solid hills jump up and down,
so wonderful it is, almighty God,
that you should come to set your people free.
As we recount your saving work,
continue to build us into the temple where you dwell
and the kingdom where you alone have dominion.
We ask this through Jesus Christ our Lord.

All   **Amen.**

tone: Joseph Gelineau

Other settings

When Israel made her way   Huijbers   OCP   L
    from Egypt

Assembly editions

Ordinary Time 1

Psalm 90 (91)

He who dwells in the shelter of the Most <u>High</u>
and abides in the shade of the <u>Al</u>mighty
say to the Lord: '<u>My</u> refuge,
my stronghold, my God in <u>whom</u> I trust!'

It is he who will free you from the <u>snare</u>
of the fowler who seeks to <u>des</u>troy you;
he will conceal you with <u>his</u> pinions
and under his wings you <u>will</u> find refuge.

You will not fear the terror of the <u>night</u>
nor the arrow that flies <u>by</u> day,
nor the plague that prowls in <u>the</u> darkness
nor the scourge that lays <u>waste</u> at noon.

A thousand may fall at your <u>side</u>,
ten thousand fall at <u>your</u> right,
you, it will never <u>a</u>pproach;
his faithfulness is buck<u>ler</u> and shield.

Your eyes have only to <u>look</u>
to see how the wicked are <u>re</u>paid,
you who have said: 'Lord, <u>my</u> refuge!'
and have made the Most <u>High</u> your dwelling.

Upon you no evil shall fall,
no plague approach where you dwell.
For you has he commanded his angels,
to keep you in all your ways.

They shall bear you upon their hands
lest you strike your foot against a stone.
On the lion and the viper you will tread
and trample the young lion
    and the dragon.

Since he clings to me in love, I will free him;
protect him for he knows my name.
When he calls I shall answer:
    'I am with you,'
I will save him in distress and give him glory.

C   With length of days I will content him;
D   I shall let him see my saving power.

Glory be to the Father, and to the Son,
and to the Holy Spirit.
As it was in the beginning, is now,
    and ever shall be,
world without end. Amen

My re-fuge, my strong-hold, my God in whom I trust!

tone: Bôquen

Presider	You, O God Most High are shade and shelter, refuge and stronghold for all who cling to you and seek to know your name. Deliver us from evil, uphold us in good works and let us see your saving power. We ask this through Jesus Christ our Lord.
All	**Amen.**

Other settings

Whoever lives	arr. Bell	PPP	P
He will conceal	Daly-Denton	L	G
Safe in the shadow	Dudley-Smith	CFE, L	P
Song of Blessing	Glynn	PS2	L
Be with me, Lord	Haugen	G, C	L
On Eagles' Wings	Joncas	G, CFE, LHON, L	L
Blest be the Lord	Schutte	CFE, LHON, L	P
Be with me, O Lord	Tamblyn	L	G

Assembly editions

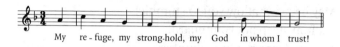

My re-fuge, my strong-hold, my God in whom I trust!

Ordinary Time 2

Psalm 120 (121)

I <u>lift</u> up my <u>eyes</u> to the <u>moun</u>tains:
from <u>where</u> shall come my <u>help</u>?
My <u>help</u> shall <u>come</u> from the <u>Lord</u>
who made <u>heaven</u> and <u>earth</u>.

May he <u>never</u> al<u>low</u> you to <u>stum</u>ble!
Let him <u>sleep</u> not your <u>guard</u>!
<u>No</u>, he <u>sleeps</u> not, nor <u>slum</u>bers,
<u>Is</u>rael's <u>guard</u>.

The <u>Lord</u> is your <u>guard</u> and your <u>shade</u>;
at your <u>right</u> side he <u>stands</u>.
By <u>day</u> the <u>sun</u> shall not <u>smite</u> you
nor the <u>moon</u> in the <u>night</u>.

The <u>Lord</u> will <u>guard</u> you from <u>evil</u>,
he will <u>guard</u> your <u>soul</u>.
The Lord will <u>guard</u> your going and <u>coming</u>
both <u>now</u> and for <u>ever</u>.

Praise to the <u>Father</u>, the <u>Son</u> and Holy <u>Spirit</u>,
both <u>now</u> and for <u>ever</u>,
the God who <u>is</u>, who <u>was</u> and who <u>will</u> be,
<u>world</u> without <u>end</u>.

Presider We look to the heights
to seek the goal of our pilgrimage,
but we find you, the Lord,
walking alongside us as we journey.
Keep us under your watchful care,
secure our life by day and night,
that we may know your unfailing protection
both now and always.
We ask this through Jesus Christ our Lord.

All **Amen.**

My help comes from God who made hea - ven and earth.

tone: Joseph Gelineau; response: A Gregory Murray OSB

Other settings

Lifting my eyes to the hills	Bell	PPP	P
I lift up my eyes	Haugen	C	L
I lift my eyes	Huijbers	CFE	L
Our helps comes from God	Joncas	G	L
In your coming	Lundy	LHON	P
I lift up my eyes	Ogden	PS3	L

Assembly editions

My help comes from God who made hea - ven and earth.

Ordinary Time 3

Psalm 109 (110):1–5, 7

The Lord's revelation to <u>my</u> Master:
'Sit on <u>my</u> right:
your foes I will put be<u>neath</u> your feet.'

The Lord will wield <u>from</u> Zion
your sceptre <u>of</u> power:
rule in the midst of <u>all</u> your foes.

A prince from the day of <u>your</u> birth
on the ho<u>ly</u> mountains;
from the womb before the dawn <u>I</u> begot you.

The Lord has sworn an oath
he will <u>not</u> change.
'You are a priest <u>for</u> ever,
a priest like Melchize<u>dek</u> of old.'

A   The Master standing at <u>your</u> right hand
C   will shatter kings in the day <u>of</u> his wrath.

A   He shall drink from the stream by <u>the</u> wayside
C   and therefore he shall lift <u>up</u> his head.

A   Glory be to the Father, and to <u>the</u> Son,
C   and to the <u>Ho</u>ly Spirit.
A   As it was in the beginning, is now,
    and <u>ev</u>er shall be,
C   world without <u>end</u>. Amen.

Presider A rightful king, a priest for ever
you give to us, O God, in Christ your Son.
Holy and splendid he is risen from death
to stand for ever at your side.
Let the whole creation
welcome the advent of his peace
and let our voices and our lives acclaim
his coming to do justice for the living and the dead,
for he lives and reigns now and for ever.

All **Amen.**

Our Sa - - viour sits at God's right hand.

tone: *Martin Foster*

Other settings

You are a priest for ever   Boulton Smith   PS3   L
The Lord said   Proulx   W   B/L

Assembly editions

Our Sa - viour sits at God's right hand.

Ordinary Time 4

Psalm 138 (139)

O Lord, you search me and <u>you</u> know me,
you know my resting and <u>my</u> rising,
you discern my purpose from <u>a</u>far.
You mark where I walk or lie down,
    all my ways lie open <u>to</u> you.

Before ever a word is on my tongue
    you know it, O Lord, through <u>and</u> through.
Behind and before you <u>be</u>siege me,
your hand ever laid <u>up</u>on me.
Too wonderful for me, this knowledge,
    too high, beyond <u>my</u> reach.

O where can I go from <u>your</u> spirit,
or where can I flee from <u>your</u> face?
If I climb the heavens you <u>are</u> there.
If I lie in the grave, you <u>are</u> there.

If I take the wings of <u>the</u> dawn
and dwell at the sea's fur<u>thest</u> end,
even there your hand <u>would</u> lead me,
your right hand would hold <u>me</u> fast.

If I say: 'Let the dark<u>ness</u> hide me
and the light around me <u>be</u> night,'
even darkness is not dark <u>for</u> you
and the night is as clear as <u>the</u> day.

For it was you who created my being,
knit me together in my mother's womb.
I thank you for the wonder of my being,
for the wonders of all your creation.

Already you knew my soul,
my body held no secret from you
when I was being fashioned in secret
and moulded in the depths of the earth.

Your eyes saw all my actions,
they were all of them written in your book;
every one of my days was decreed
before one of them came into being.

To me, how mysterious your thoughts,
the sum of them not to be numbered!
If I count them, they are more than the sand;
to finish, I must be eternal, like you.

O search me, God, and know my heart.
O test me and know my thoughts.
See that I follow not the wrong path
and lead me in the path of life eternal.

Glory be to the Father, and to the Son,
and to the Holy Spirit.
As it was in the beginning,
    is now, and ever shall be,
world without end. Amen.

O search me, God, and know my heart.

tone: Tamié

Presider	Creator God,
	with you the darkness is not dark,
	with you the night is radiant as the day.
	By that light search us out,
	test and judge the thoughts and ways
	of those whose inmost heart you know,
	so that we may shun the crooked paths
	and follow you along your ancient way.
	We ask this through Jesus Christ our Lord.
All	**Amen**

Other settings

O God, you search me	Farrell	CBOL, L, PS3	P
You are near	Schutte	CFE, LHON, L	P
You know me, Lord	Walsh	L	L

Assembly editions

O search me, God, and know____ my heart.

SUPPLEMENT

Notes

This supplement of four psalms is provided for those communities who wish to use a richer diet of psalmody. The four psalms could be used in a number of ways:

- one could be used as a second psalm, sung after the seasonal psalm if required – on particular occasions, Solemnities, for example;
- some communities may wish to complement the constant seasonal psalm with a changing second psalm to add variety;
- the four psalms provided could be used in rotation through the year – 116: week 1, 113b: week 2 etc.;
- the inclusion of these psalms means that *Celebrating Sunday Evening Prayer* can also be used as a resource for those who wish to follow the provision in the *Divine Office*.

The setting of Psalm 116 (117) can also be used as a simple common tone and response.

Common Tone and Response

The two-line tone and 'Alleluia' response used for Psalm 116 (page 83) can replace the given psalm tone and response for any of the psalms. It is offered for those communities which wish to sing the psalms using a tone but do not wish to begin by having to learn a new tone every season.

- The two-line tone is repeated in four-line verses.
- In Lent the 'Alleluia' response is not used. The response 'With the Lord' (page 69) can be used with this tone.

Supplementary Psalm I

Psalm 116 (117)

O praise the Lord, <u>all</u> you nations,
acclaim him <u>all</u> you peoples!

Strong is his <u>love</u> for us;
he is faith<u>ful</u> for ever.

Praise the Father, the Son and <u>Ho</u>ly Spirit,
both now and for ever, world <u>with</u>out end.

Presider Faithful God,
we thank you for the gift of your Son, Jesus Christ,
may his love be made known throughout the world
so that all may come to praise your name.
We ask this through Christ our Lord.

All **Amen.**

Al - le - lu - ia, al - le - lu - ia, al - le - lu - ia!

response: A Gregory Murray OSB

Other settings

Praise your maker	Bell	PPP	P
Go to all the world	Haas	G	L
Go out to the whole world	Jakob	PBTC, C	L
Holy is God	Inwood	HIG, L	L
Alleluia, praise the Lord	O'Carroll	MMII, L	L
Come, praise the Lord	Quinn	CFE, LHON, L	P
Laudate Dominum	Taizé	CFE, LHON, L	O
Laudate omnes gentes	Taizé	LHON, L	O
Alleluia, praise the Lord	Walker	SS3, MMII	L

Assembly editions

Al - le - lu - ia, al - le - lu - ia, al - le - lu - ia!

Supplementary Psalm II

Psalm 113b (115)

Not to us, Lord, <u>not</u> to us,
but to your name <u>give</u> the glory
for the sake of your love <u>and</u> your truth,
lest the heathen say: 'Where <u>is</u> their God?'

But our God is <u>in</u> the heavens;
he does whatev<u>er</u> he wills.
Their idols are sil<u>ver</u> and gold,
the work of <u>hu</u>man hands.

They have mouths but they <u>can</u>not speak;
they have eyes but they <u>can</u>not see;
they have ears but they <u>can</u>not hear;
they have nostrils but they <u>can</u>not smell.

With their hands they <u>can</u>not feel;
with their feet they <u>can</u>not walk.
No sound comes <u>from</u> their throats.
Their makers will come to be like them
    and so will all who <u>trust</u> in them.

Sons of Israel, trust <u>in</u> the Lord;
he is their help <u>and</u> their shield.
Sons of Aaron, trust <u>in</u> the Lord;
he is their help <u>and</u> their shield.

You who fear him, trust <u>in</u> the Lord;
he is their help <u>and</u> their shield.
He remembers us, and he will bless us;
    he will bless the <u>sons</u> of Israel.
He will bless the <u>sons</u> of Aaron.

The Lord will bless <u>those</u> who fear him,
the little no less <u>than</u> the great:
to you may the Lord <u>grant</u> increase,
to you and <u>all</u> your children.

May you be blessed <u>by</u> the Lord,
the maker of he<u>aven</u> and earth.
The heavens belong <u>to</u> the Lord
but the earth he has <u>given</u> to men.

The dead shall not <u>praise</u> the Lord,
nor those who go down <u>into</u> the silence.
But we who live <u>bless</u> the Lord
now and for <u>ever</u>. Amen.

Glory be to the Father, and to <u>the</u> Son,
and to the Ho<u>ly</u> Spirit.
As it was in the beginning,
    is now, and <u>ever</u> shall be,
world without end. <u>A</u>men.

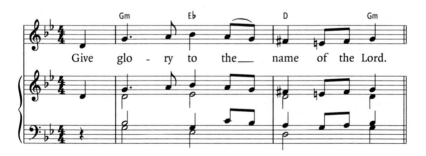

Give glo - ry to the___ name of the Lord.

Presider　　　God of truth and love
　　　　　　　you sent your Son to come among us as a man
　　　　　　　so that we might know God with us,
　　　　　　　Jesus whom we have have seen and heard,
　　　　　　　and who gave his live for us.
　　　　　　　Through him we sing your praise
　　　　　　　for ever and ever.
All　　　　　　**Amen.**

Assembly editions

Give glo - ry to the___ name of the Lord.

Supplementary Psalm III

Psalm 110 (111)

I will thank the Lord with <u>all</u> my heart
in the meeting of the just and <u>their</u> assembly.
Great are the works <u>of</u> the Lord;
to be pondered by <u>all</u> who love them.

Majestic and glor<u>ious</u> his work,
his justice stands <u>firm</u> for ever.
He makes us remem<u>ber</u> his wonders.
The Lord is compas<u>sion</u> and love.

He gives food to <u>those</u> who fear him;
keeps his covenant <u>ever</u> in mind.
He has shown his might <u>to</u> his people
by giving them the lands <u>of</u> the nations.

His works are just<u>ice</u> and truth:
his precepts are all <u>of</u> them sure,
standing firm for <u>ever</u> and ever:
they are made in upright<u>ness</u> and truth.

A   He has sent deliverance <u>to</u> his people
B   and established his cove<u>nant</u> for ever.
D   Holy his name, <u>to</u> be feared.

A   To fear the Lord is the first <u>stage</u> of wisdom;
B   all who do so prove <u>themselves</u> wise.
D   His praise shall <u>last</u> for ever!

Glory be to the Father, and to the Son,
and to the Holy Spirit.
As it was in the beginning,
    is now, and ever shall be,
world without end. Amen.

Presider   God of compassion and love
you keep your promise to feed those
who fear your name.
May we come to know you more and more
so that we may praise your glorious works.
We ask this through Christ our Lord

All   **Amen**

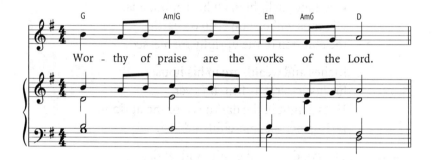

Wor - thy of praise are the works of the Lord.

Assembly editions

Wor - thy of praise are the works of the Lord.

Supplementary Psalm IV

Psalm 111 (112)

Happy the man who <u>fears</u> the Lord,
who takes delight in all <u>his</u> commands.
His sons will be power<u>ful</u> on earth;
the children of the up<u>right</u> are blessed.

Riches and wealth are <u>in</u> his house;
his justice stands <u>firm</u> for ever.
He is a light in the darkness <u>for</u> the upright:
he is generous, mer<u>ciful</u> and just.

The good man takes pi<u>ty</u> and lends,
he conducts his af<u>fairs</u> with honour.
The just man will <u>never</u> waver:
he will be remem<u>bered</u> for ever.

He has no fear of <u>evil</u> news;
with a firm heart he trusts <u>in</u> the Lord.
With a steadfast heart he <u>will</u> not fear;
he will see the downfall <u>of</u> his foes.

A   Open-handed, he gives <u>to</u> the poor;
B   his justice stands <u>firm</u> for ever.
D   His head will be <u>raised</u> in glory.

A   The wicked man sees <u>and</u> is angry,
B   grinds his teeth and <u>fades</u> away;
D   the desire of the wicked <u>leads</u> to doom.

Glory be to the Father, and to the Son,
and to the Holy Spirit.
As it was in the beginning,
    is now, and ever shall be,
world without end. Amen.

Presider

God of the faithful and the just
you sent your Son to be a light
to all who take delight in your commands.
May we learn to follow your ways
so that we may bless your name for ever.
We ask this through Christ our Lord.

All

Amen

Let your light shine and give glo - ry to God.

Assembly editions

Let your light shine and give glo - ry to God.

New Testament Canticle

The ways of performing the canticle are similar to those mentioned in the section on the psalms (page 55).

The canticle from Revelation is sung throughout the year except in the season of Lent when it is replaced by the text from the first letter of Peter.

If the canticle is not sung it may be omitted.

Settings

Revelation 19:1-2, 5-7

1   Simple tone 1

Salvation, glory and power be<u>long</u> to our God.
His judgements are <u>true</u> and just.
Alleluia, Alleluia, Alleluia!

Praise our God, <u>you</u> his servants.
You who fear him, <u>small</u> and great.
Alleluia, Alleluia, Alleluia!

The Lord our God the al<u>might</u>y reigns.
Let us rejoice and exult and <u>give</u> him the glory.
Alleluia, Alleluia, Alleluia!

The marriage of the <u>Lamb</u> has come,
And his bride has <u>made</u> herself ready.
Alleluia, Alleluia, Alleluia!

Praise to the Father, Son and Ho<u>ly</u> Spirit,
both now and for ages unend<u>ing</u>. Amen.
Alleluia, Alleluia, Alleluia!

Simple tone 1 and 2 Music: Chant/ Martin Foster

2   Simple tone 2

Alleluia, Alleluia, Alleluia!

Salvation, glory and power be<u>long</u> to our God. **Alleluia!**
His judgements are <u>true</u> and just. **Alleluia!**
Praise our God, <u>you</u> his servants. **Alleluia!**
You who fear him, <u>small</u> and great. **Alleluia ...**

The Lord our God the al<u>mighty</u> reigns. **Alleluia!**
Let us rejoice and exult and <u>give</u> him the glory. **Alleluia!**
The marriage of the <u>Lamb</u> has come, **Alleluia!**
And his bride has <u>made</u> herself ready. **Alleluia ...**

Glory be to the Father and <u>to</u> the Son, **Alleluia!**
and to the Ho<u>ly</u> Spirit. **Alleluia!**
As it was in the beginning, is now, and <u>ever</u> shall be, **Alleluia!**
world without <u>end</u>. Amen. **Alleluia ...**

3 Andrew Wright

'Alleluia' is sung first by the cantor and repeated by all each time. The verses are sung in the manner of a Gelineau psalm – to a regular pulse. [–] indicates an omitted bar.

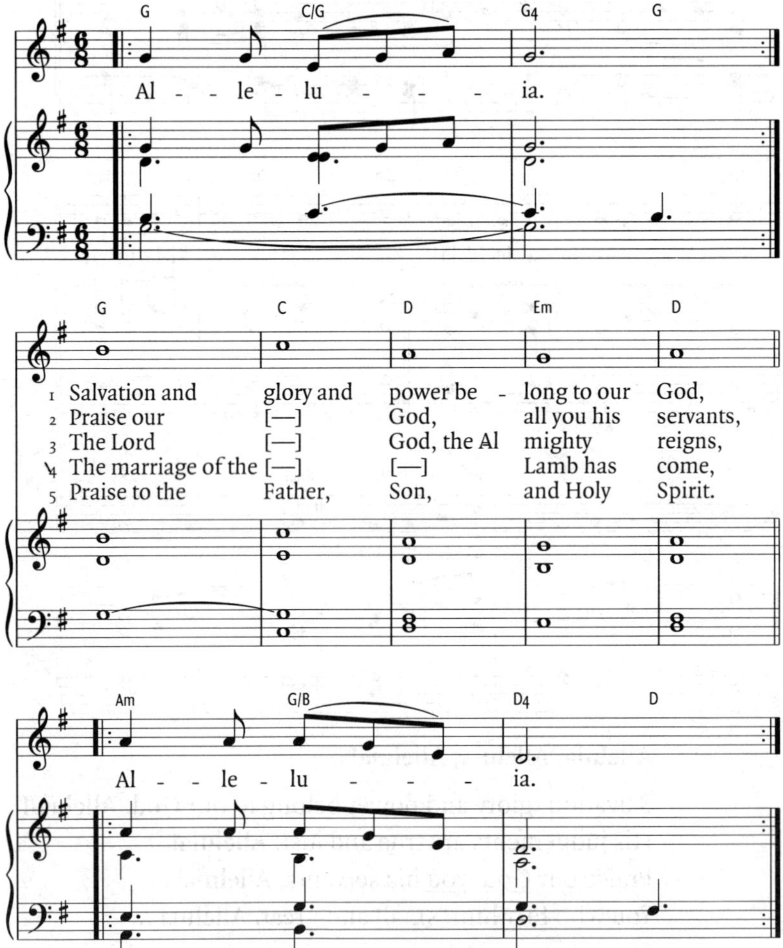
G C/G G4 G
Al - - le - lu - - - ia.
G C D Em D
1 Salvation and glory and power be - long to our God,
2 Praise our [—] God, all you his servants,
3 The Lord [—] God, the Al mighty reigns,
4 The marriage of the [—] [—] Lamb has come,
5 Praise to the Father, Son, and Holy Spirit.
Am G/B D4 D
Al - - le - lu - - - ia.

His judgements are true and [—] just.
You who fear him, small and great.
Let us re - - joice ex - - ult and give glory.
And his bride has made herself ready.
Both now and for ages un - - ending. A - - men.

Al - - le - lu - - - ia.

music: Andrew Wright

1 Peter 2:21–24

for use in the season of Lent

4   Laurence Bévenot OSB

By his wounds we have been healed.

Christ suffered for you, leaving you <u>an</u> example
that you should follow <u>in</u> his steps.
He committed no sin; no guile was found <u>on</u> his lips.
When he was reviled, he did not revile <u>in</u> return.

When he suffered, he <u>did</u> not threaten;
but trusted to him who <u>ju</u>dges justly.
He himself bore our sins in his body <u>on</u> the tree,
that we might die to sin and <u>live</u> to righteousness.

tone: *Laurence Bévenot* OSB; *response: Martin Foster*

Other settings

Revelation 19:1–2, 5–7

Rev 19	Daly	AA	L
Rev 19	Dean	CFE, L	L
Rev 19	Wright	MM	L

1 Peter 2:21–24

As prophets foretold	Jones	L, PBTC	L
Ours were the griefs	Dean	CFE, L	L

Assembly editions

1 Simple Tone 1

2 Simple Tone 2

3 Andrew Wright

Al - le - lu - - ia.

Al - le - lu - - ia.

Al - le - lu - - ia.

4 Laurence Bévenot OSB

By his wounds we have been healed.

Word

Structure

Word

Scripture Reading

Response

Magnificat

Scripture Reading

The scripture reading at Evening Prayer is a time for reflection on the Word of God. At Evening Prayer it should usually be:

- from either the Old or New Testament excluding the Gospels.
- of moderate length and reflect the liturgical seasons.

It is recommended that the second reading of the Sunday eucharist is either repeated or use made of that given in the Lectionary for another liturgical year (e.g., in year A using the second readings of year B or C in the Lectionary cycle). This would give a pattern to the readings over a year and would also give a second hearing to a reading which is often neglected.

Performance

The reading may take place at a lectern, the ambo or from the reader's place, depending on the setting and the nature and scale of the assembly. It may help lead into silence if 'This is the word of the Lord' is omitted.

The reading should be proclaimed with a clear voice and be followed with sufficient time for reflection. The text should be read from a bible or a lectionary.

Response

A time of silence after the reading allows time for reflection on the scripture. If desired it can be followed either by a brief homily or reflection, or by the reflective singing of a chant. The chant may pick up the reading or the broader themes of the liturgical season.

Settings

Behold the Lamb of God	Iona	Advent	CAYP, CFE, L
Veni Immanuel	Iona	Advent	CAYP
Wait for the Lord	Taizé	Advent	CFE, LHON, L
Adoramus te	Taizé	Christmas	CFE, LHON, L
He became poor	Iona	Christmas	CFE, L
Word of the Father	Iona	Christmas	CAYP, L
Bless the Lord	Taizé	Lent	CFE, LHON, L
Stay with me	Taizé	Lent	LHON, L
Alleluia Fontium	Inwood	Easter	WAYP, MFM
Confitemini Domino	Taizé	Easter	CFE, LHON, L
Pour out, I will pour out	Iona	Easter	CAYP
Surrexit Christus	Taizé	Easter	CFE, LHON, L
Laudate omnes gentes	Taizé		CFE, LHON, L
In the Lord	Taizé		CFE, LHON, L
O Christe Domine Jesu	Taizé		CFE, LHON, L
Your word, O Lord	Taizé		C

My Spirit rejoices in GOD my Saviour

Magnificat

Luke 1:46–55

- All stand for the Gospel Canticle. Incense may be burned.

The ways of singing the Magnificat are similar to those mentioned in the section on the psalms (page 49).

My soul glorifies the Lord,
my spirit rejoices in God, my Saviour,
He looks on his servant in her lowliness;
henceforth all ages will call me blessed.

The Almighty works marvels for me.
Holy his name!
His mercy is from age to age,
on those who fear him.

He puts forth his arm in strength
and scatters the proud-hearted.
He casts the mighty from their thrones
and raises the lowly.

He fills the starving with good things,
sends the rich away empty.

He protects Israel, his servant,
remembering his mercy,
the mercy promised to our fathers,
to Abraham and his sons for ever.

Settings

1   JP Lécot (Lourdes)

Mag - ni - fi - cat, mag - ni - fi - cat   a - ni - ma me - a Do - mi - num!

1 My   soul   glorifies the   Lord,
     He   looks on his   servant in her   lowliness;
2 The Al - mighty works   marvels for   me.
     His   mercy is from   age to   age,
3 He   puts forth his   arm in   strength
     He   casts the   mighty from their thrones

my   spirit re - joices in   God, my   Saviour,
hence - forth all   ages will   call me   blessed.
     [—]   [—]   Holy his   name!
on   [—]   [—]   those who   fear him.
and   [—]   [—]   scatters the proud - hearted.
and   [—]   [—]   raises the   lowly.

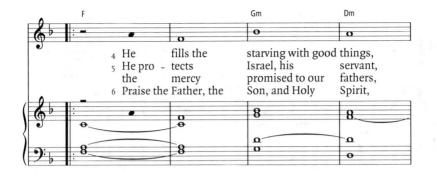

4 He   fills the   starving with good things,
5 He pro - tects   Israel, his   servant,
   the   mercy   promised to our   fathers,
6 Praise the Father, the   Son, and Holy   Spirit,

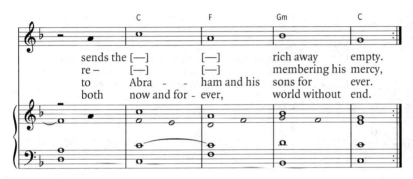

sends the [—]   [—]   rich away   empty.
re –   [—]   [—]   membering his mercy,
to   Abra - - ham and his sons for   ever.
both   now and for - ever,   world without end.

music: Jean-Paul Lécot

2 *Joseph Gelineau*

The Lord has done mar-vels for me: ho-ly is his name.

1 My soul glorifies the Lord,
He looks on his servant in her nothingness;
5 the mercy promised to our fathers,
Praise the Father, the son and Holy Spirit,

my spirit re - joices in God, my Saviour.
hence-forth all ages will call me blessed.
to Abra - - ham and his sons for ever.
both now and for ever, world without end.

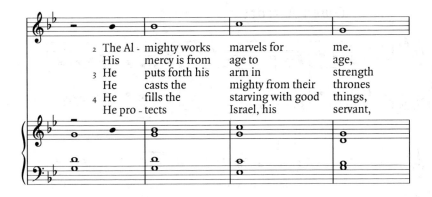

2 The Al - mighty works marvels for me.
  His mercy is from age to age,
3 He puts forth his arm in strength
  He casts the mighty from their thrones
4 He fills the starving with good things,
  He pro - tects Israel, his servant,

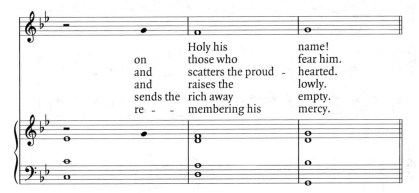

on Holy his name!
those who fear him.
and scatters the proud - hearted.
and raises the lowly.
sends the rich away empty.
re - - membering his mercy.

music: Joseph Gelineau

3   Owen Alstott

My soul re - joi - ces   in the

My soul re - joi - ces   in God, my_ Sav - iour.

Lord!   In_ God,_ my

My spi - rit finds its joy in God, the liv - ing

text and music: Owen Alstott

vv. 1 – 5 | Final

God. _____   God. _____

God. _____   God. _____

1 My soul pro - claims your migh - ty deeds. My
2 Your mer - cy flows through-out the land and
3 You cast the migh - ty from their thrones and
4 You fill the hun - gry with good things. With
5 Just as you prom - ised A - bra - ham, you

spi - rit sings the great-ness of your name.
ev - ery gen - er - a - tion knows your love.
raise the poor and low - ly to new life.
emp - ty hands you send the rich a - way.
come to free your peo - ple, Is - ra - el.

D.S.

4 Bernadette Farrell

day a - bove all oth - ers fa - voured me and raised me
love and mer - cy sure I will pro - claim for all who
kings will swift - ly fall from thrones cor - rupt, the strong brought
- el, as once fore-told to Ab - ra - ham, will live in
Ho - ly Spi - rit, gen - tle Com - fort - er, all glo - ry

up, a light for all to see.
know and praise God's ho - ly name.
low, the low - ly lift - ed up.
peace through-out the pro-mised land.
be, both now and ev - er - more.____

text: Owen Alstott; music: Bernadette Farrell

5 Anne Carter

1 My soul proclaims you, mighty God,
my spirit sings your praise.
You look on me, you lift me up,
and gladness fills my days.

2 All nations now will share my joy;
your gifts you have outpoured.
Your little one you have made great;
I magnify my God.

3 For those who love your holy name,
your mercy will not die.
Your strong right arm puts down the proud
and lifts the lowly high.

4 You fill the hungry with good things,
the rich you send away.
The promise made to Abraham
is filled to endless day.

5 Then let all nations praise our God,
the Father and the Son,
the Spirit blest who lives in us,
while endless ages run.

text: Anne Carter;
tune: CM (Common Metre)
including Belmont, Billing, St Magnus and Tallis' Ordinal

Other settings

My soul is filled with joy	Anon	CFE, LHON, L	P
Magnificat	Boyce	RS	L
My soul rejoices	Dean	VE	L
Tell out my soul	Dudley-Smith	CFE, LHON, L	P
Sing my soul	Foster	C	P
Great is the Lord	Inwood	WAYP, CFE, L	P
My soul rejoices	Jones	VE	L
The Almighty works marvels	Jones	L, MFM2	O
God fills me with joy	Lécot	LHON	L
Magnificat	Plainchant	JD	
My soul proclaims	Sosa	VE	L
Magnificat (canon)	Taizé	SPT, LHON, L	O
Magnificat (chorale)	Taizé	SPT, C	O

Assembly editions

1 J P Lécot (Lourdes)

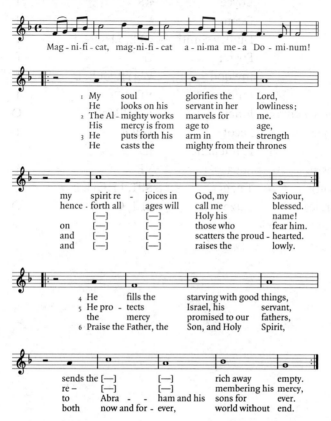

Mag - ni-fi - cat, mag-ni-fi - cat   a - ni-ma me - a Do - mi-num!

1 My	soul	glorifies the	Lord,
He	looks on his	servant in her	lowliness;
2 The Al -	mighty works	marvels for	me.
His	mercy is from	age to	age,
3 He	puts forth his	arm in	strength
He	casts the	mighty from their thrones	

my	spirit re -	joices in	God, my	Saviour,
hence - forth all	ages will		call me	blessed.
	[—]	[—]	Holy his	name!
on	[—]	[—]	those who	fear him.
and	[—]	[—]	scatters the proud -	hearted.
and	[—]	[—]	raises the	lowly.

4 He	fills the	starving with good things,	
5 He pro - tects		Israel, his	servant,
the	mercy	promised to our	fathers,
6 Praise the Father, the		Son, and Holy	Spirit,

sends the [—]	[—]	rich away	empty.
re –	[—]	[—]	membering his mercy,
to	Abra - - ham and his	sons for	ever.
both	now and for - ever,	world without	end.

2 Joseph Gelineau

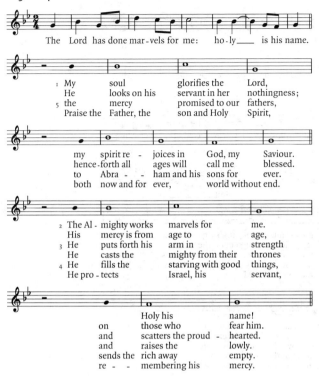

The Lord has done mar-vels for me: ho-ly___ is his name.

1 My soul glorifies the Lord,
He looks on his servant in her nothingness;
5 the mercy promised to our fathers,
Praise the Father, the son and Holy Spirit,

my spirit re - joices in God, my Saviour.
hence-forth all ages will call me blessed.
to Abra - - ham and his sons for ever.
both now and for ever, world without end.

2 The Al - mighty works marvels for me.
His mercy is from age to age,
3 He puts forth his arm in strength
He casts the mighty from their thrones
4 He fills the starving with good things,
He pro - tects Israel, his servant,

Holy his name!
on those who fear him.
and scatters the proud - hearted.
and raises the lowly.
sends the rich away empty.
re - - membering his mercy.

(Accompaniment)

My soul re - joi - ces___ in God, my_ Sav - iour.

My spi - rit finds its joy in God, the liv - ing

_vv. 1 - 5_ | Final

God.___ God.___

1 My soul pro - claims your migh - ty deeds. My
2 Your mer - cy flows through-out the land and
3 You cast the migh - ty from their thrones and
4 You fill the hun - gry with good things. With
5 Just as you prom - ised A - bra - ham, you

D.S.

spi - rit sings the great-ness of your name.
ev - ery gen - er - a - tion knows your love.
raise the poor and low - ly to new life.
emp - ty hands you send the rich a - way.
come to free your peo - ple, Is - ra - el.

4 Bernadette Farrell

1 My soul pro-
2 Through me great
3 God's migh-ty
4 Soon will the
5 All Glo-ry

claims the great-ness of the Lord.   My spi-rit
deeds will God make ma-ni-fest,   and all the
arm, pro-tec-tor of the just,   will guard the
poor and hun-gry of the earth   be rich-ly
be to God, Cre-a-tor blest,   to Je-sus

sings to God, my sav-ing God,   who on this
earth will come to call me blest.   Un-bound-ed
weak and raise them from the dust.   But migh-ty
blest, be giv-en great-er worth.   And Is-ra-
Christ, God's love made ma-ni-fest,   and to the

day a-bove all oth-ers fa-voured me and raised me
love and mer-cy sure I will pro-claim for all who
kings will swift-ly fall from thrones cor-rupt, the strong brought
-el, as once fore-told to Ab-ra-ham, will live in
Ho-ly Spi-rit, gen-tle Com-fort-er, all glo-ry

vv.1-4 D.S.

up,   a light for all to see.
know   and praise God's ho-ly name.
low,   the low-ly lift-ed up.
peace   through-out the pro-mised land.
be,   both now and ev-er-more.

© 1993, Bernadette Farrell and Owen Alstott. Published by OCP.

Prayer

Structure

Prayer

Intercessions

Lord's Prayer

Concluding Prayer and Blessing

Intercessions

Intercessions should lead to prayer, they are invitations to pray, not the prayer itself. Although examples are provided, groups are encouraged to compose their own, following the guidelines below. Spontaneous prayer may also be included. It is simple and effective to invite people to pray their own petitions but in the style of the prepared intercessions. The sequence given in the *General Instruction of the Roman Missal* is a useful starting point: for the needs of the Church, for public authorities and the salvation of the world, for those oppressed by any need, for the local community (GIRM 70).

- The form should be: *intention – silent prayer – response.*
- The intention should be brief, inclusive and invite prayer, e.g., *For the sick.* rather than *Let us pray for the sick of our parish who are ill at this time: for Mrs Jones, Mr Smith, Sr Mary...* Depending on the size of the group it may be sensitive to invite people to name people who are sick or to take another example name parts of the world that are longing for Christ's peace.
- The last intercession at Evening Prayer is traditionally for the dead.
- The intercessions are led by a second reader from the lectern, ambo or the assembly.

- Singing the response highlights the importance of prayer in the Liturgy of the Hours. The response may be intoned by a cantor and repeated by all. The intercessions may also be sung.

The intentions of these sample intercessions are based on the Cycle of Prayer (see Appendix 2).

The Intercessions can be taken from the *Divine Office*.

Other settings

Through our lives	Bell	CFE, L
God our Father	Dean	C
Loving Father	Dean	C
Give peace in our time	Foster	C
Hear our prayer	Hurd	C
Lord, in your mercy	Inwood	CFE
We ask you, Lord	Inwood	L
God ever faithful	Joncas	L
O God, hear us	Walker	C

ADVENT

Reader   We pray to the Lord, who is, who was and who is to come:

Pause for silent prayer.

All   **Come, Lord Jesus! Come, quickly come.**

Reader   John the Baptist heralded your coming;
  we pray for all who preach the Good News:

  For all who work for justice and peace:

  For all who are rejected by society:

  For all who are expecting the birth of a child:

Additional intentions, names, and commemorations are included here.

  For the dead, who await your coming in glory:

CHRISTMAS

Reader Let us pray to the Father through Christ the Word made flesh:

Pause for silent prayer.

All **Lord, be with your people.**

Reader The angels sang of peace on earth;
 teach us all the ways of peace:

 We pray for refugees
 and for all who live away from their native land:

 We remember the lives of innocent children,
 who die every day:

 We pray for families, in their joy and in their pain:

 We remember the lonely and the unloved:

Additional intentions, names, and commemorations are included here.

 We pray for those who have died at this time;
 that they may be reborn into the kingdom of Heaven:

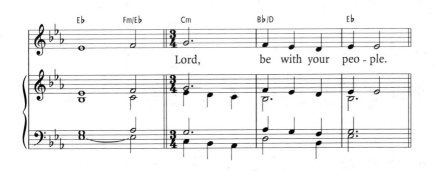

LENT

Reader   Christ prayed for forty days in the desert,
as we continue our Lenten journey
we make our prayers known to the Father of all mercies:

Pause for silent prayer.

All   **Hear our prayer and have mercy.**

Reader   That we may be renewed in Christ:

                  For all those preparing for the Easter sacraments:

                  For freedom from sin and a change of heart.:

                  For all in this world who hunger and thirst:

                  For all who give their lives for others:

Additional intentions, names, and commemorations are included here.

                  For all who sleep in Christ and await his resurrection:

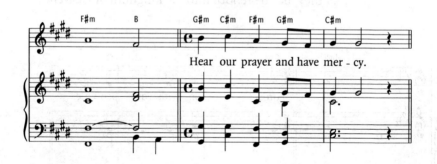

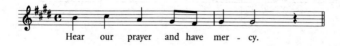

EASTER

Reader   We pray to the Father through Christ,
                who is risen in glory at God's right hand:

Pause for silent prayer.

All   **Christ is our light and our joy.**

Reader   For the Church of God throughout the world:

                For the newly baptised
                and all received into the Church at Easter:

                For openness to the call of God
                and for a spirit of discernment:

                For all those preparing for First Holy Communion:

Additional intentions, names, and commemorations are included here.

                For the dead, the first fruits of Christ's resurrection:

ORDINARY TIME 1

Reader   Through Christ we make our prayers known to the Father:

Pause for silent prayer.

All   **Teach us your ways, Lord.**

Reader   For the Christian church in all its diversity:

For peace in lands torn by war and conflict:

For the sick and for those who care for them:

For teachers, students and all engaged in education:

Additional intentions, names, and commemorations are included here.

For all those whose anniversary occurs at this time:

ORDINARY TIME 2

Reader   In trust and hope we turn to the Father:

Pause for silent prayer.

All   **Lord, all our hope is in you.**

Reader   For the spiritual growth of our parish community:

      For all who work and for all who seek work:

      For all who suffer persecution for belief:

      For all who travel:

      For families:

Additional intentions, names, and commemorations are included here.

      For all who have died recently:

ORDINARY TIME 3

Reader   We pray to the Lord in confidence and trust.

Pause for silent prayer.

All   **We pray to the Lord.**

Reader   For all who care for others in their work:

               For peace and understanding between nations:

               For all who care for God's creation:

               For fairness and equality for all in society:

Additional intentions, names, and commemorations are included here.

               For all the faithful departed:

ORDINARY TIME 4

Reader   In prayer we address our needs to God:

Pause for silent prayer.

All   **Your kingdom come, O Lord.**

Reader   For all who preach the Good News of Christ:

                 For the stewardship of the earth:

                 For victims of war and injustice:

                 For all who suffer in mind or body:

Additional intentions, names, and commemorations are included here.

                 For the dying and all who care for them:

                 For all who have died, remembered or forgotten:

Your
Kingdom
come
O
Lord.

Lord's Prayer

At the conclusion of the intercessions the presider introduces the Lord's Prayer which is said by all. The doxology may be added. The prayer may be sung, though other items have greater priority for singing, such as hymns, psalms, canticles.

The Lord's Prayer may be followed by an invitation to share a sign of peace.

The prayer may be introduced in these or similar words.

Advent
Presider   Lord, as we look forward to the coming of the Kingdom,
                  teach us to pray:

Christmas
Presider   Rejoicing in the presence of God here among us,
                  let us pray in faith and hope:

Lent
Presider   In a spirit of forgiveness we say together:

Easter
Presider   Together with the newly baptised
                  let us pray as Christ taught us:

Ordinary Time
Presider   With confidence we pray to the Father
                  in the words our Saviour gave us:

Settings
   1 Laurence Bévenot   134
   2 Rimsky-Korsakov   136

Other Settings

Lord's Prayer	Duffy	L
Pater noster	chant	JD, L, C

Music settings

1   *Laurence Bévenot* OSB

Our Father, who art in heaven, hal-lowed be thy name.

Thy kingdom come. Thy will be done on earth, as it is in heaven.

Give us this day our dai-ly bread, and forgive us our trepasses;

as we forgive those who tres-pass a-gainst us,

and lead us not into temp-ta-tion, but de-li-ver us from e-vil.

music: *Laurence Bévenot* OSB

Our Father, who art in heaven, hal-lowed be thy name.

Thy kingdom come. Thy will be done on earth, as it is in heaven.

Give us this day our dai - ly bread, and forgive us our trepasses;

as we forgive those who tres - pass a - gainst us,

and lead us not into temp-ta-tion, but de - li - ver us from e - vil.

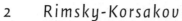

2 Rimsky-Korsakov

Our Fa-ther, who art in heaven, hal-lowed be thy name; thy king-dom come; thy will be done on earth as it is in heaven. Give us this day our dai-ly bread; and for-give us our tres-pas-ses as we for-give those who tres-pass a-gainst us. And lead us not in - to temp - ta - tion, but de - li - ver us from e - vil.

music: Rimsky-Korsakov

Assembly editions

Our Fa-ther, who art in heaven, hal-lowed be thy name; thy king-dom

come; thy will be done on earth as it is in heaven.

Give us this day our dai-ly bread; and for-give us our tres-pas-ses

as we for-give those who tres-pass a-gainst us. And lead us not

in - to temp-ta-tion, but de - li - ver us from e - vil.

Concluding Prayer

The concluding prayer and blessing are led by the presider.

Concluding Prayer texts
- The Concluding Prayer can be taken from the *Divine Office*.

ADVENT

A
God our Father,
you overcame the stubbornness of human hearts,
and their resistance to your call,
as you prepared the coming of the Messiah.
Grant that we too may be faithful
and persevere to the end in the ways that you have called us,
and in waiting for him who is to come,
Jesus, our Lord.

B
God, Lord of Eternity,
your Son came to visit us in time.
Grant to each of us the heart of a child
which never ceases to marvel at your wonders,
so that once again this evening,
you may find us watching in hope.
We ask you this, because of your love for us,
God blessed for ever and ever.

CHRISTMAS

A
Loving Father,
your final word to us is your Word incarnate;
Grant that we may welcome him with all our hearts,
respond in love to your unending love,
and gain eternal life, through Christ, our Lord.

B
Lord God, Friend of all who live,
at the evening of this day
we commit to you the suffering of the poorest.
Grant that they may hope in him
who became one of them.
For he brings them deliverance
and desires to fill them with your riches,
who lives and reigns with you
and the Holy Spirit, for ever and ever.

LENT

A
Lord our God,
by the death and resurrection of your Son Jesus,
you have given life to the world.
In this time of Lent,
inspire and accept our efforts at penance and sharing.
Bring all people into the fullness of your life,
through Jesus, the Christ, our Lord.

B
God our Father,
you have given the good things of this day
to the upright and to sinners alike.
Teach us to be merciful like you
and to forgive whole-heartedly.
So shall we be ready to receive your salvation,
through Jesus, the Christ, our Lord.

EASTER

A
Blessed be you, Lord Jesus Christ,
you have walked with us this day,
sharing your Word and your Living Bread.
Stay with us now as evening falls;
that the joy of your presence
may burn in our hearts
for you are our light,
for ever and ever.

B
Father of our Lord Jesus Christ,
in the evening of the Resurrection,
you brought the disciples together
to reveal to them the presence of your Son.
May the Good News of his victory
be heard by all your people,
so that all may come together and see his face,
who lives for ever and ever.

ORDINARY TIME

A
Ever faithful God,
you love us and bless us in Jesus Christ your Son.
By him alone you are perfectly glorified.
At this evening hour,
may your Spirit in us
sing the marvels of your salvation;
God most high,
who lives for ever and ever.

B
In the peace of evening,
we come to you, Lord God.
May your Word free our hearts
from the cares of this day.
As we experience your forgiveness in Jesus,
may we too forgive in him
our brothers and sisters who have injured us.
We ask this in his name,
Jesus, the Christ, our Lord.

C   It is for you that we live, Lord our God,
and to you we have consecrated this day;
perfect and purify our offering,
so that our prayer of thanksgiving
may rise to you,
in Jesus, your Son, our Lord.

D   Lord God, ever faithful,
see us gathered before you
as the day draws to a close;
confirm our hearts in your love,
and keep alive in us
the memory of your goodness and kindness,
which have appeared in Jesus Christ, our Lord.

E   Lord our God,
you called us to begin this day.
Now at its ending our tasks lie incomplete,
our hopes are not achieved.
Grant that we may be with you
where our weakness will be overcome,
and all our longing be fulfilled,
in Jesus, your Son, our Lord.

F   Lord our God,
this day is drawing to a close,
At the hour of evening sacrifice
you gather us in praise.
Keep us from, all anxiety,
and stir up in our hearts a longing for your day.
Hear us in the love you bear us,
through Christ and the Holy Spirit,
for ever and ever.

Blessing

A   *An ordained presider*

Presider	The Lord be with you.
All	**And also with you.**
Presider	May almighty God bless you, the Father, and the Son, and the Holy Spirit.
All	**Amen.**

B   *A lay presider*

Presider	The Lord bless us, and keep us from all evil, and bring us to everlasting life.
All	**Amen.**

APPENDICES

APPENDIX 1
PLANNING SHEET

Celebrating Sunday Evening Prayer

Season   ....

Presider   ....

Other Ministers   ....

                                   ....

                                   ....

                                   ....

Introduction

Opening Responses – Hymn   ☐
Hymn – Opening Responses   ☐

Opening Responses   A   ☐   B   ☐

Hymn   ....

                                   ....

                                   ....

                                   ....

Light   ☐   Incense   ☐   Thanksgiving ☐

Light   ....

    Collect   ....

Incense   ....

    Collect   ....

Thanksgiving   ....

Psalmody

Psalm ....

....

Supplementary
Psalm ....

Canticle ....

Word

Word ....

....

....

....

....

Response ....

....

Magnificat ....

Prayer

Intercessions ....

Response ....

Lord's Prayer ....

Concluding Prayer ....

This planning sheet may be freely copied.

APPENDIX 2
CALENDAR

Solemnities and Feasts of the Lord that are celebrated on Sundays for England and Wales

Advent

First Sunday of Advent	27 November – 3 December

Christmas

Christmas Day	25 December
Holy Family	26–31 December
Mary, Mother of God	1 January
Second Sunday after Christmas	2–4 January
Epiphany of the Lord	5–7 January
Baptism of the Lord	8–13 January

Ordinary Time [I]

Presentation of the Lord	2 February

Lent

Easter

Pentecost	

Ordinary Time [II]

Trinity Sunday	
Birth of St John the Baptist	24 June
St Peter and St Paul	28–30 June

Ordinary Time [III]

Transfiguration of the Lord	6 August
Assumption of the Blessed Virgin Mary	14–16 August
Triumph of the Cross	14 September

Ordinary Time [IV]

All Saints	31 October – 2 November
Dedication of the Lateran Basilica	9 November

See *www.liturgyoffice.org.uk/Calendar for up-to-date calendar information.*

CYCLE OF PRAYER

*During the Seasons of the Cycle of Prayer the following themes are prayed for.
Many of these intentions also have a particular day associated with them.*

Advent/Christmas

Migrants and Refugees
> Migrants' Day: *3 December*

Openness to the Word of God
> Bible Sunday: *Second Sunday of Advent*

Expectant Mothers
> Expectant Mothers: *especially on Fourth Sunday of Advent*

Ordinary Time – Winter

Peace on Earth
> Day for Peace: *Second Sunday in Ordinary Time*

Christian Unity
> Octave of Prayer for Christian Unity: *18–25 January*

The Sick and Those Who Care for Them
> World Day for the Sick: *11 February (Our Lady of Lourdes)*

Students and Teachers
> Education Day: *three Sundays before First Sunday of Lent*

The Unemployed
> Day for the Unemployed: *Sunday before First Sunday of Lent*

Lent

Candidates for the Sacraments

> Candidates for the Sacraments: *especially on the Sundays of Lent*

Women

> Women's World Day of Prayer: *first Friday in March*

The Needy and Hungry of the World

> Lent Fast Day: *Friday in the first week of Lent*

Penitents and Wanderers

Easter

New Members of the Church

Vocations

> World Day of Prayer for Vocations: *Fourth Sunday of Easter*

The Right Use of the Media

> World Communications Day: *Sunday after Ascension*

Human Work

> St Joseph the Worker: *1 May*

The Church

> The Church: *especially at Pentecost*

Ordinary Time – Summer

A Deeper Understanding between Christians and Jews

Those Who Suffer Persecution, Oppression and Denial of Human Rights
        St John Fisher and St Thomas More: *22 June*

Europe

        Europe: St Benedict, St Brigid and St Benedicta as below
           also SS Cyril and Methodius (*14 February*)
           and St Catherine of Siena (*29 April*).
        St Benedict: *11 July*
        St Brigid: *23 July*
        St Benedicta of Cross: *9 August*

Human Life

        Day for Life: *First Sunday in July*

Seafarers

        Sea Sunday: *Second Sunday in July*

Ordinary Time – Autumn

Justice and Peace in the World
        Racial Justice Day: *second Sunday in September*
        Harvest Fast Day: *first Friday in October*

The Spread of the Gospel
        Home Mission Day: *third Sunday in September*
        World Mission Day: *penultimate Sunday in October*

The Harvest; the Fruits of Human Work, and the Reverent Use of Creation;
        The Harvest, etc: *Sunday between 22–28 September*
          or whenever Harvest Festivals are held

All Victims of War
        Remembrance Day: *Second Sunday in November*

Young People
        Youth Day: *Christ the King*

Prisoners and their Families
        Prisoners' Week: *9–15 November*
        Day of Prayer for Prisoners: *Third Sunday in November*
          and their Dependants

APPENDIX 3
MODEL LITURGIES

Introduction

This section presents two liturgies compiled from the resources in this book. The aim is to show how this material might be used. Both a complete text and a model leaflet is offered. The first liturgy is a simple celebration for Advent; the second, a full celebration of Evening Prayer for Easter Sunday. At the end of this section there is a description of how a parish might begin celebrating Evening Prayer simply and develop it over time.

Advent Evening Prayer
- text   151
- leaflet   156

This Evening Prayer is for a small group just starting – see longer description on page 172. The prayer is led by a deacon and there is also a reader. Only the hymn and the Magnificat are sung. The leaflet is used over the four weeks of Advent with a different hymn being chosen for each week.

Evening Prayer for Easter Sunday
- text   160
- leaflet   166

This Evening Prayer is planned as a solemn celebration to mark the end of the Easter Triduum. It involves many ministers and much singing. There is a procession and use of both light and incense.

Commentary

ADVENT EVENING PRAYER

Introduction

Opening Responses

Presider	O God, come to our aid.
All	**O Lord, make haste to help us.**
Presider	Glory be to the Father, and to the Son and to the Holy Spirit,
All	**as it was in the beginning,**
	is now and ever shall be world without end. Amen.
	Alleluia.

Hymn

1 Come, thou long-expected Jesus,
born to set thy people free,
from our fears and sins release us,
let us find our rest in thee.

2 Israel's strength and consolation,
hope of all the earth thou art;
dear desire of every nation,
joy of every longing heart.

3 Born thy people to deliver,
born a child and yet a king,
born to reign in us for ever,
now thy gracious kingdom bring.

4 By thine own eternal Spirit
rule in all our hearts alone;
by thine all-sufficient merit
raise us to thy glorious throne.

Charles Wesley (1707–88)

Brief word of welcome.

Thanksgiving

Presider	Let us give thanks to the Lord our God.
All	**It is right to give him thanks and praise.**
Presider	Blessed are you, Sovereign God, creator of light and darkness! As evening falls, you renew your promise to reveal among us the light of your presence. May your word be a lantern to our feet and a light upon our path, that we may behold your glory coming among us. Strengthen us in our stumbling weakness and free our tongues to sing your praise, Father, Son and Holy Spirit:
All	**Blessed be God forever!**

Psalmody

Psalm 84

The psalm is recited antiphonally.

> O Lord, you once favoured your land
> and revived the fortunes of Jacob,
> you forgave the guilt of your people
> and covered all their sins.
> You averted all your rage,
> you calmed the heat of your anger.
>
> Revive us now, God, our helper!
> Put an end to your grievance against us.
> Will you be angry with us for ever,
> will your anger never cease?
>
> Will you not restore again our life
> that your people may rejoice in you?
> Let us see, O Lord, your mercy
> and give us your saving help.

I will hear what the Lord has to say,
a voice that speaks of peace,
peace for his people and his friends
and those who turn to him in their hearts.
His help is near for those who fear him
and his glory will dwell in our land.

Mercy and faithfulness have met;
justice and peace have embraced.
Faithfulness shall spring from the earth
and justice look down from heaven.

The Lord will make us prosper
and our earth shall yield its fruit.
Justice shall march before him
and peace shall follow his steps.

Glory be to the Father and to the Son
and to the Holy Spirit.
As it was in the beginning, is now,
    and ever shall be,
world without end. Amen

a period of silence.

Psalm Prayer

Presider   Revive us now, God our helper!
restore us to fullness of life in you;
that mercy and truth may be our guide
and peace be a pathway for our feet.
We ask this through Jesus Christ our Lord.

Word

Scripture Reading
1 Thessalonians 3:12 – 4:2

followed by a period of silence.

Magnificat

1   Tell out, my soul, the greatness of the Lord!
Unnumbered blessings, give my spirit voice;
tender to me the promise of his word;
in God my Saviour shall my heart rejoice.

2   Tell out, my soul, the greatness of his name!
Make known his might, the deeds his arm has done;
his mercy sure, from age to age the same;
his holy name, the Lord, the Mighty One.

3   Tell out, my soul, the greatness of his might!
Powers and dominions lay their glory by.
Proud hearts and stubborn wills are put to flight,
the hungry fed, the humble lifted high.

4   Tell out, my soul, the glories of his word!
Firm is his promise, and his mercy sure.
Tell out, my soul, the greatness of the Lord
to children's children and for evermore!

Timothy Dudley-Smith

Prayer

Intercessions

The presider invites people to name concerns for the world, the Church and the local community. The following response is used

Presider	Lord, in your mercy.
All	**Hear our prayer.**

Lord's Prayer

Presider	Lord, as we look forward to the coming of the Kingdom, teach us to pray.
All	**Our Father...**

Concluding Prayer

Presider   God our Father,
you overcame the stubbornness of human hearts,
and their resistance to your call,
as you prepared the coming of the Messiah.
Grant that we too may be faithful
and persevere to the end in the ways that you have called us,
and in waiting for him who is to come,
Jesus, our Lord.

We make our prayer...

Blessing

Presider	The Lord be with you.
All	**And also with you.**
Presider	May almighty God bless you, the Father, and the Son and the Holy Spirit.
All	**Amen.**

Magnificat
Tell out my soul (in hymn book)

All stand.

Intercessions
Lord, in your mercy.

All   **Hear our prayer.**

Lord's Prayer

Concluding Prayer

Blessing

Presider   The Lord be with you.

All   **And also with you.**

Presider   May almighty God bless you,
the Father, and the Son and the Holy Spirit.

All   **Amen.**

Acknowledgements Texts from *The Divine Office* © The hierarchies of Australia, England & Wales, Ireland and Scotland. Psalm © 1963 The Grail (England).

4

ADVENT EVENING PRAYER

Opening Responses

All stand

Presider	O God, come to our aid.
All	**O Lord, make haste to help us.**
Presider	Glory be to the Father, and to the Son and to the Holy Spirit,
All	**as it was in the beginning,**
	is now and ever shall be world without end. Amen.
	Alleluia.

Hymn

from hymn book

Thanksgiving

Presider	Let us give thanks to the Lord our God.
All	**It is right to give him thanks and praise.**
Presider	Blessed are you, Sovereign God,
	creator of light and darkness...
	...Father, Son and Holy Spirit:
All	**Blessed be God forever!**

1

Psalm 84

All sit

The psalm is recited antiphonally.

A   O Lord, you once favoured your land
and revived the fortunes of Jacob,
you forgave the guilt of your people
and covered all their sins.
You averted all your rage,
you calmed the heat of your anger.

B   Revive us now, God, our helper!
Put an end to your grievance against us.
Will you be angry with us for ever,
will your anger never cease?

Will you not restore again our life
that your people may rejoice in you?
Let us see, O Lord, your mercy
and give us your saving help.

I will hear what the Lord has to say,
a voice that speaks of peace,
peace for his people and his friends
and those who turn to him in their hearts.
His help is near for those who fear him
and his glory will dwell in our land.

2

Mercy and faithfulness have met;
justice and peace have embraced.
Faithfulness shall spring from the earth
and justice look down from heaven.

The Lord will make us prosper
and our earth shall yield its fruit.
Justice shall march before him
and peace shall follow his steps.

Glory be to the Father and to the Son
and to the Holy Spirit.
As it was in the beginning, is now,
    and ever shall be,
world without end. Amen

The psalm is followed by a period of silence and a psalm prayer.

Scripture Reading

The reading is followed by a period of silence.

3

EASTER SUNDAY
EVENING PRAYER

The Easter Candle is lit.

Introduction

Hymn
Sing of one who walks beside us

All stand.
There is a procession of ministers.

Opening Responses

Presider	Jesus Christ, risen in glory, you are the light of the world:
All	**the light no darkness can overcome;**
Presider	Stay with us now, for it is evening,
All	**and the day is almost over.**
Presider	Let your light scatter the darkness,
All	**and shine among your people here.**

Light Service

During the singing of the response members of the assembly light their candles.

The Lord is my light, my light and sal-va-tion: in him I trust, in him I trust. The

Thanksgiving

Presider	Let us give thanks to the Lord our God
All	**It is right to give him thanks and praise.**
Presider	Blessed are you, Sovereign God,
	our light and our salvation;
	to you be glory and praise for ever!
	You led your people to freedom
	by a pillar of cloud by day
	and a pillar of fire by night,
	May we who walk in the light of your presence
	acclaim your Christ, rising victorious,
	as he banishes all darkness from our hearts and minds,
	and praise you, Father, Son and Holy Spirit:
All	**Blessed be God for ever!**

Psalmody

Psalm 113a

All sit.

The psalm is sung antiphonally.

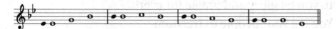

When Israel came forth from Egypt,
Jacob's sons from an alien people,
Judah became the Lord's temple,
Israel became God's kingdom.

The sea fled at the sight,
the Jordan turned back on its course,
the mountains leapt like rams
and the hills like yearling sheep.

Why was it sea, that you fled,
that you turned back, Jordan, on your course?
Mountains that you leapt like rams;
hills, like yearling sheep?

Tremble, O earth, before the Lord,
in the presence of the God of Jacob,
who turns rock into a pool
and flint into a spring of water.

Give praise to the Father Almighty,
to his Son, Jesus Christ, the Lord,
to the Spirit who dwells in our hearts,
both now and for ever. Amen.

a period of silence

Presider   As if rivers should run backwards
or the solid hills jump up and down,
so wonderful it is, almighty God,
that you should come to set your people free.
As we recount your saving work,
continue to build us into the temple where you dwell
and the kingdom where you alone have dominion.
We ask this through Jesus Christ our Lord.

Psalm 116

sung responsorially.

O praise the Lord, <u>all</u> you nations,
acclaim him <u>all</u> you peoples!

Strong is his <u>love</u> for us;
he is faith<u>ful</u> for ever.

Praise the Father, the Son and <u>Ho</u>ly Spirit,
both now and for ever, world <u>with</u>out end.

Presider   Faithful God,
we thank you for the gift of your Son, Jesus Christ,
may his love be made known throughout the world
so that all may come to praise your name.
We ask this through Christ our Lord.

Canticle
Revelation 19

During the singing of the canticle all process to the font.
Setting 3 – Wright is sung (page 74).

Word

Scripture Reading
Romans 6:3–11

The reading is followed by a period of silence.

Response
During the singing of the chant Confitemini Domino people are invited to bless themselves with water from the font.

Magnificat
During the singing of the Magnificat incense is burned.
Setting 3 – Alstott is sung (page 112).

Prayer

Intercessions

Reader   We pray to the Father through Christ,
                    who is risen in glory at God's right hand:
Pause for silent prayer.

All   Christ is our light and our joy.

Reader   For the Church of God throughout the world:

                   For the newly baptised
                   and all received into the Church this Easter:

                   For all who serve the community through liturgical ministry:

                   For the peace of the risen Christ to touch all people:

Additional intentions, names, and commemorations are included here.

                   For the dead, the first fruits of Christ's resurrection:

Lord's Prayer

Presider	Together with the newly baptized let us pray as Christ taught us:
All	**Our Father...**

Concluding Prayer

Presider	Father of our Lord Jesus Christ, in the evening of the Resurrection, you brought the disciples together to reveal to them the presence of your Son. May the Good News of his victory be heard by all your people, so that all may come together and see his face, who lives for ever and ever.

Blessing

Presider	The Lord be with you.
All	**And also with you.**
Presider	May almighty God bless you, the Father, and the Son and the Holy Spirit.
All	**Amen.**

Leaflet 166–171

As the liturgy has many parts the leaflet runs over six sides. As a model leaflet here it has been run continuously, rather than as it would be rearranged for printing on two sheets of A4.

Easter Sunday
Evening Prayer

Hymn

1 Sing of one who walks beside us
and this day is living still,
one who now is closer to us
than the thoughts our hearts distil,
one who once upon a hilltop,
raised against the pow'r of sin,
died in love as his own creatures
crucified their God and King!

2 Strangers we have walked beside him
the long journey of the day,
and have told him of the darkness
that has swept our hope away.
He has offered words of comfort,
words of energy and light,
and our hearts have blazed within us
as he saved us from the night.

3 Stay with us, dear Lord, and raise us,
once again the night is near.
Dine with us and share your wisdom,
free our hearts from ev'ry fear.
In the calm of each new evening,
in the freshness of each dawn,
if you hold us fast in friendship
we will never be alone.

Ralph Wright OSB

1

Opening Responses

Presider   Jesus Christ, risen in glory,
you are the light of the world:

All   **the light no darkness can overcome;**

Presider   Stay with us now, for it is evening,

All   **and the day is almost over.**

Presider   Let your light scatter the darkness,

All   **and shine among your people here.**

Light Service

During the singing of the response members of the assembly light their candles.

The Lord is my light, my light and sal-va-tion: in

him I trust, in him I trust. The

Thanksgiving

Presider   Let us give thanks to the Lord our God.

All   **It is right to give him thanks and praise.**

Presider   Blessed are you, Sovereign God,
our light and our salvation...

... Father, Son and Holy Spirit:

All   **Blessed be God forever!**

2

Psalm 113a

All sit
The psalm is sung antiphonally.

When Israel came forth from Egypt,
Jacob's sons from an alien people,
Judah became the Lord's temple,
Israel became God's kingdom.

The sea fled at the sight,
the Jordan turned back on its course,
the mountains leapt like rams
and the hills like yearling sheep.

Why was it sea, that you fled,
that you turned back, Jordan, on your course?
Mountains that you leapt like rams;
hills, like yearling sheep?

Tremble, O earth, before the Lord,
in the presence of the God of Jacob,
who turns rock into a pool
and flint into a spring of water.

Give praise to the Father Almighty,
to his Son, Jesus Christ, the Lord,
to the Spirit who dwells in our hearts,
both now and for ever. Amen.

The psalm is followed by a period of silence and a psalm prayer.

3

Psalm 116

The psalm is sung responsorially.

Al - le - lu - ia, al - le - lu - ia, al - le - lu - ia!

Canticle – Revelation 19

During the singing of the canticle all process to the font.
Repeat Alleluia after the cantor.

Al - le - lu - - - ia.

Al - le - lu - - - ia.

Al - le - lu - - - ia.

Scripture Reading
Romans 6:3–11

The reading is followed by a period of silence.

4

Response

Con-fi-te-mi-ni Do-mi-no quo-ni-am bo-nus.

Con-fi-te-mi-ni Do-mi-no, Al-le-lu - ia!

Magnificat

(Accompaniment)

My soul re - joi - ces____ in God, my_ Sav - iour.

My spi - rit finds its joy in God, the liv - ing

vv. 1 - 5 | Final

God.____ God.____

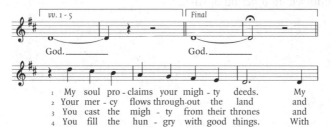

1 My soul pro - claims your migh - ty deeds. My
2 Your mer - cy flows through-out the land and
3 You cast the migh - ty from their thrones and
4 You fill the hun - gry with good things. With
5 Just as you prom - ised A - bra - ham, you

D.S.

spi - rit sings the great-ness of your name.
ev - ery gen - er - a - tion knows your love.
raise the poor and low - ly to new life.
emp - ty hands you send the rich a - way.
come to free your peo - ple, Is - ra - el.

5

Intercessions

Christ is our light and our joy.

Lord's Prayer

Concluding Prayer

Blessing

Presider	The Lord be with you.
All	**And also with you.**
Presider	May almighty God bless you,
	the Father, and the Son and the Holy Spirit.
All	**Amen.**

Acknowledgements Texts from *The Divine Office* © The hierarchies of Australia, England & Wales, Ireland and Scotland; *The Lord is my light* by Jacques Berthier © Ateliers et Presses de Taizé; *Sing of one* by Ralph Wright OSB © GIA Publications; Psalm © 1963 The Grail (England); Rev 19 © Andrew Wright; *Confitemini Domino* © Ateliers et Presses de Taizé; *My soul rejoices* by Owen Alstott © 1984, 1991 OCP Publications; excerpts from *Celebrating Sunday Evening Prayer* copyright © 2006 Catholic Bishops' Conference of England and Wales.

6

COMMENTARY

This section offers a narrative of how one community might use this resource. It starts simply with Advent and describes how they develop their celebration of Evening Prayer over a year.

Advent

After attending a formation day on Evening Prayer run by the diocese the parish liturgy group decided to start celebrating Evening Prayer in Advent. A few years before they had ceased to have a Mass on Sunday evening and so now nothing regularly happened in the church on Sunday afternoon. They began preparation and decided to start simply. They used a simple form of Evening Prayer at the meetings they had so that they would get use to the rhythm and pattern of it. The parish deacon was asked to lead the liturgy and the group identified people to prepare the environment and to read. Though a musician was not available they still planned to sing the hymn and Magnificat – they were used to unaccompanied singing from the weekday Mass. A leaflet was prepared which covered all four weeks of Advent.

Advent
Opening Responses B
Hymn
Thanksgiving
Psalm 84
Reading
Magnificat – *Tell out my soul*
Intercessions
Lord's Prayer
Concluding Prayer and Blessing

On the first Sunday fifteen people came. Afterwards they said they appreciated the simplicity of the celebration and the space for silent prayer and reflection. Beforehand the first candle on the Advent Wreath had been lit and people were invited to place incense on the charcoals during the Intercessions. Though the group wanted the prayer to be inviting they thought it should have a formality about it so the deacon vested in an alb. Before the celebration there was a short introduction by one of the group. This explained the overall structure and said that the hope was to continue every Sunday. Some elements would be repeated every week so that people began to know them and enter into the prayer. The psalm was read each week – the preparation group had decided that it should be read with a measured pace with a slight pause between the verses. Members of the group positioned themselves on both sides of the congregation to achieve this. For the reading, which was read from the ambo, they had decided to follow the suggestion of using the previous year's second reading from Sunday Mass. The intercessions were spontaneous. They were introduced by the deacon who invited people to use a simple form – and members of the preparation group had been asked to be prepared to offer intercessions for the first few weeks to give people confidence. Numbers fluctuated over the four weeks but there were never less than ten people there.

Christmas

When they began preparing to celebrate Evening Prayer the group looked ahead to have an idea about how they would plan the coming year. One thing they immediately realised is that it might be difficult to celebrate over the Christmas Season. That year Christmas Day was on a Wednesday so they thought that it would be possible to celebrate on the following Sunday – the feast of the Holy Family and then on the Epiphany.

Christmas

Opening Responses B
Hymn – *Carol*
Thanksgiving

Psalm 23

Reading
Magnificat – *Tell out my soul*

Intercessions
Lord's Prayer
Concluding Prayer and Blessing

In the event twelve people came, some of them new – they welcomed something being on at church and that it offered some quiet space.

To make the environment more festive not only was the Advent Wreath lit but other candles were lit before the liturgy around the church. They had decided to keep the same pattern of celebration as Advent: they sang a carol for the hymn and continued using *Tell out my soul* as a setting of the Magnificat. The Thanksgiving, the psalm and the intercessions were changed with the season.

After the celebration on Epiphany they decided to have some refreshments to mark Twelfth Night.

Ordinary Time 1

At an early stage the parish liturgy group realised that it would not be fair to rely on the parish deacon to preside every week at Evening Prayer. The parish priest took Monday as his day off and was often gone by Sunday afternoon. So, two of the group offered to attend a training course for lay presiders that the diocese was offering.

Ordinary Time 1
  Opening Responses B
  Hymn
  Light
  Thanksgiving
  Psalm 90
  Reading
  Magnificat – *Tell out my soul*
  Intercessions
  Lord's Prayer
  Concluding Prayer and Blessing

The pattern of the liturgy remained much the same, but they used a different thanksgiving and intercessions. They considered using a four-week cycle of the psalms of Ordinary Time but after a short discussion realised that they had come to appreciate the repetition week by week. To mark the dark winter months they lit candles around the worship space during a period of silence after the hymn. Outside the seasons of Advent and Christmas they found it harder to find hymns that they were all confident singing every week. It was decided for the hymn to create a four-week cycle – they thought the hymn was one part where they would appreciate some variety every week.

Lent

Now that they had been celebrating Evening Prayer as a parish since Advent the liturgy group thought that it would be good to take stock of what they had achieved and how they wanted the liturgy to develop. The pair who had been on the leader's training course told the group that a simple form of Evening Prayer (similar to what they had been doing in the parish) had been part of the training sessions. One of them found it reassuring to pray in a similar way outside the parish. Her previous experience of the Office has been using books with ribbons where you had to keep your fingers in different places to say the prayer and though she found the parish celebrations prayerful she had not been quite sure it was the prayer of the Church. Both of them remarked that on the training course they had appreciated the singing of the psalms to a simple tone and they were sure that they could manage it. The rest of the group agreed that this was an obvious way for the celebration to develop although they were less confident. It was decided to see if any of the parish cantors would come and help them for Lent to start them off. Two of the cantors offered to help every other week but they gradually found themselves coming every week to pray. After a bit of thought they decided to sing both the psalm and the New Testament canticle. They sang them both to the same psalm tone and sang them all together rather than dividing into two sides.

Lent

Opening Responses B
Hymn
Incense
Thanksgiving
Psalm 129
Canticle – 1 Peter
Reading
Magnificat – *Tell out my soul*
Intercessions
Lord's Prayer
Concluding Prayer and Blessing

Incense was used at the beginning of the liturgy rather than light and they placed incense on the charcoal as a silent response to the intercessions. As part of the liturgy group's reflection they had recognised that Lent would be another opportunity to invite members of the parish to the celebration. They made a special effort to invite those preparing for baptism at Easter and even when they were unable to come each week remembered them in their prayers.

The two lay leaders each led Evening Prayer twice during Lent. Though they realised that on paper there was not much for them to do they gave a good amount of time to preparing together so that they would be able to lead with confidence. Unlike the parish deacon they decided not to wear an alb and, as was their usual practice for Celebrations of the Word and Communion, they did not use the presider's chair. They sat in the front bench and moved out to stand on the sanctuary step when they had to preside.

Easter
The preparation group had decided not to celebrate Evening Prayer on Easter Sunday as they guessed that they would all be exhausted by the Easter Triduum. In the event a number of people commented the next week that they had missed the opportunity to pray and reflect quietly

about the previous few days. The group realised that this would be something they had to consider for next year.

Easter
Opening Responses B
Hymn
Light
Thanksgiving

Psalm 113a
Canticle – Rev. 19

Reading
Magnificat – *Tell out my soul*

Intercessions
Lord's Prayer
Concluding Prayer and Blessing

When they began singing the psalm during Lent the preparation group realised that once they had started it would be counter-productive to revert to saying it – particularly in the Easter season. To build on what they had achieved they used the same psalm tone as they had used in Lent with Psalm 113a and continued to sing it all together. The canticle from Revelation was more of a challenge. Though the cantors wanted to try the third setting as they thought it was the more joyful setting, in the end they used the second setting. When neither of the cantors could be there on the Sixth Sunday of Easter the group could sing the psalm confidently by themselves and for the Canticle they used the Alleluia refrain, which they also used at weekday Mass, with a single reader proclaiming the verses.

Otherwise much was the same as it had been in the preceding months – many of them hardly looked at their books for the Introduction and the Magnificat. As it was Easter they used the paschal candle, already lit at the beginning of the liturgy, as the focus for their prayer and the source of light. On Pentecost Sunday they managed to process the Candle to beside the font while they sang the Magnificat. As on Epiphany they decided to mark the end of the season with some refreshments.

Ordinary Time 2

It was realised that over the summer months that attendance would fluctuate. At the refreshments after the Pentecost Evening Prayer people were asked if they wanted to stop for July and August. Overwhelmingly people said they hoped that the Prayer would continue and they would make an effort to attend – the prayer had become part of the rhythm of their week.

Ordinary Time 2
Opening Responses B
Hymn
Thanksgiving

Psalm 120
Canticle – Rev. 19

Reading
Magnificat – *Tell out my soul*

Intercessions
Lord's Prayer
Concluding Prayer and Blessing

Leaders, cantors, readers and those who prepared the liturgical space were asked to indicate when they would not be able to come. The deacon and the two lay leaders met together to look at what was possible as they recognised that some weeks decisions would have to be made depending on who was there. Their intention was to maintain their current practice: to have a four-week cycle of hymns as they had used in January and February; to sing the psalm to the tone they had learnt in Lent; they would also use incense during the intercessions as they had in Lent. They looked at various scenarios and decided if there was nobody to lead the music they would, if necessary, omit the hymn and maybe place some incense on the charcoal in silence before the Thanksgiving. They would have a go at singing the psalm and the Magnificat; for the canticle from Revelation they would repeat what they had done once in the Easter Season and sing the 'Alleluia' and have the text proclaimed.

Over the summer numbers kept to around ten, though occasionally they were visitors who said afterwards how they had appreciated it and wished their parish did something similar. In the event they found that they could continue singing, even in the weeks when neither of the cantors could come and they were few in number. There was not only a corporate memory but a corporate confidence too.

Ordinary Time 3

As Easter had been late that year Ordinary Time had not started until the middle of June. The group therefore decided to continue using their Ordinary Time 2 choices for August and September. At first they considered just continuing into August but they thought that it would be counter-productive to change texts just for one month.

In September one of the regular group died after a short illness. He had asked that Evening Prayer be celebrated on the evening before the funeral at the reception of the body. Many who came found the liturgy very moving.

Ordinary Time 4

For October and November they made seasonal changes: they continued to use the same tone for the psalm.

On Remembrance Sunday they decided to mark November with a special Evening Prayer for the Dead to which they invited not only members of the parish but families of those who had been bereaved in the last year. To mark the occasion they invited people to come forward and for each to light a candle in the Introductory Rites as the names of those who had died in the last year were read out. They decided to use an additional psalm and picked Psalm 129, which they had used in Lent, as the first psalm. The parish music group were invited to help and they taught everyone a simple response about light which was used both as the candles were lit and after the reading. The music group wanted to replace the psalm tones with versions of the psalm they were familiar with but the preparation group were keen that liturgy should reflect how they normally celebrated. Once again there was an opportunity for refreshments afterwards.

Ordinary Time 4

Opening Responses B

Hymn

Thanksgiving

Psalm 138

Canticle – Rev. 19

Reading

Magnificat – *Tell out my soul*

Intercessions

Lord's Prayer

Concluding Prayer and Blessing

For the Dead

Opening Responses B

Hymn

Light

Thanksgiving

Psalm 129

Psalm 138

Canticle – Rev. 19

Reading

Magnificat – *Tell out my soul*

Intercessions

Lord's Prayer

Concluding Prayer and Blessing

Looking forward

The parish had now been celebrating Sunday Evening Prayer for a year. Though numbers fluctuated there was now a core of twenty people with three people trained to lead the prayer and the services of three cantors. It was seen as a valuable addition to the prayer life of the parish; those who came worked hard to make sure that it did not become a group activity but was seen as the prayer of the Church.

Towards the end of the year the parish liturgy group who had worked with the smaller preparation group had a discussion about how the celebration should develop. There was a general feeling, though people were surprised how far they had come since their first fumbling attempts last Advent, that any development should be taken slowly. They recognised the need to perhaps use a second psalm tone and also to try another version of the Magnificat. One of the cantors had seen that there was a simple setting of the text with a psalm tone in the hymn book which they might try. After a year of trying various options they needed to consider how best to mark the liturgical seasons: when to use light and incense; if they had two psalm tones which psalms would they use them for. It was also wondered if they might use a more formal style of intercessions – when there were a larger number of people the individual prayers were often indistinct. The parish liturgy group suggested that Sunday Evening Prayer in Christian Unity week might be an occasion to invite members of other churches to attend. The group also began to reflect on how they could celebrate Evening Prayer on Easter Sunday.

APPENDIX 4
LIST OF ABBREVIATIONS

AA	Alleluia, Amen (Veritas)
AK	Acclaim the King (McCrimmons)
C	Cantate (Decani)
CAYP	Come all you people (Iona)
CBOL	Christ, be our light (OCP)
CFE	Celebration Hymnal for Everyone (McCrimmons)
CTSF	Come to set us free (OCP)
G	Gather (GIA)
HIG	Holy is God (OCP)
LHON	Liturgical Hymns Old and New (Mayhew)
JD	Jubilate Deo (CTS)
L	Laudate (Decani)
MFM	Music for the Mass (Chapman)
MFM2	Music for the Mass 2 (Chapman)
OCP	Octavo (OCP)
PBTC	Praise be to Christ (OCP)
PPP	Psalms of Prayer, Protest and Praise (Iona)
PS1–3	Psalm Songs 1–3 (Chapman)
RS	Rejoice 'n' Sing 1 (CJM)
SPT	Songs and Prayers from Taizé (Mowbray)
SS3	Songs of the Spirit 3 (Mayhew)
VE	Veni Emmanuel (Decani)
W	Worship (GIA)
WAYP	We are your people (OCP)

BIBLIOGRAPHY

Ritual Books

The Divine Office: 3 Volumes, (HarperCollins: London 1974).
The complete text of the Divine Office is available in 3 volumes. Various shorter one-volume editions have been extracted from it:
> *Daily Prayer* – Morning, Midday and Evening Prayer through the year, (HarperCollins: London 1980).
> *Morning and Evening Prayer* – Morning and Evening Prayer through the year, (HarperCollins: London 1976).
> *Shorter Morning and Evening Prayer* – omits Commemoration of Saints, (HarperCollins: London 1983).

Book of Blessings, (Liturgical Press: Collegeville 1989).
This *Book of Blessings* is approved for use in England and Wales.

Holy Communion and Worship of the Eucharist outside Mass, (John F Neale: Evesham 1978).

Lectionary (Volume 1), (Chapman: London 1983 – ritual edition; Harper Collins: London 1983 – study edition).

Order of Christian Funerals, (Geoffrey Chapman: London 1990).

General Introduction

Liturgy Documents: Volume 2 includes General Introduction to the Liturgy of the Hours, (LTP: Chicago 1999).

A M Roguet: *Liturgy of the Hours: General Instruction with Commentary,* (Liturgical Press: Collegeville 1986).

Commentaries and Studies

Paul Bradshaw, *Two Ways of Praying: Introducing Liturgical Spirituality,* (SPCK: London 1995).

Paul Bradshaw, *Daily Prayer in the Early Church,* (OUP: Oxford 1982).

Stanislaus Campbell FSC: *From Breviary to Liturgy of the Hours: The Structural Reform of the Roman Office 1964–1971*, (Pueblo: Collegeville 1995).

J D Crichton, *Christian Celebration: Understanding the Prayer of the Church*, (Geoffrey Chapman: London 1993).

Austin Flannery, *Companion to the new Breviary*, (Dominican Publications: Dublin 1997).

John Gallen, ed., *Christians at Prayer*, (Notre Dame: University of Notre Dame Press 1977).

George Guiver, *Company of Voices: Daily Prayer and the People of God*, (London: SPCK 1988; 2nd edn, Norwich: Canterbury Press 2001).

Robert Taft SJ: *The Liturgy of the Hours in East and West*, (Liturgical Press: Collegeville 1986).

Gregory Woolfenden, *Daily Prayer: Origins and Theology*, (Ashgate: Aldershot 2004).

Joyce Ann Zimmerman, *Morning and Evening Prayer: A Parish Celebration*, (LTP: Chicago 1996).

Text Resources

The Grail Psalms, (HarperCollins: London 1966, 2003).

Common Worship: Daily Prayer, (Church House Publishing: London 2002).

Proclaiming all your wonders: Prayers for a Pilgrim People, (Dominican Publications: Dublin 1991).

Bruce Carlin, Tom Jamieson, *Daily Prayer: A form of prayer and praise for use at any time of day*, (DLT: London 2002).

Alan Griffiths, *Celebrating the Christian Year*, (Canterbury Press, Norwich 2004).

Brian Magee, *Psalm Prayers for Morning and Evening* (Veritas: Dublin 1991).

John Allyn Melloh, William G Storey, *Praise God in Song: Ecumenical Daily Prayer*, (GIA Publications: Chicago 1979).

Society of St Francis, *Celebrating Common Prayer*, (Mowbray: London 1992).

Joyce Ann Zimmerman et al *Pray without ceasing: Prayer for Morning and Evening*, (Liturgical Press: Collegeville 1995).

Hymn Books

Office Hymns

Hymns for Prayer and Praise, (Canterbury Press: Norwich 1996).

Hymnal for the Hours, (GIA Publications: Chicago 1989).

General Hymnbooks

Celebration Hymnal for Everyone, (McCrimmons: Great Wakering 1994).

Laudate: a hymn book for the liturgy, (Decani Music: Mildenhall 1999).

Liturgical Hymns Old and New, (Kevin Mayhew: Stowmarket 1999).

Other hymnbooks

Gather, (GIA publications: Chicago 2nd edition 1994).

Worship, (GIA publications: Chicago 3rd edition 1986).

Music Resources

Psalters and Music for the Office

The Responsorial Psalter ed. Stephen Dean, (McCrimmons: Great Wakering 1997).

Psalms for Sundays, Andrew Moore, (Kevin Mayhew: Stowmarket 1997).

Tones for the Office, Laurence Bévenot, (Parish Music: Liverpool).

A collection of Psalm Tones, Panel of Monastic Musicians.

Music for Evening Prayer, Alan Rees, (Kevin Mayhew: Stowmarket 2001).

General Music Resources

Alleluia, Amen, ed. Margaret Daly, (Veritas: Dublin 1983).

Acclaim the King, ed Chris O'Hara, (McCrimmons: Great Wakering 1986).

Cantate, ed. Stephen Dean, (Decani Music: Brandon 2004).

Christ, be our light, Bernadette Farrell, (OCP: Portland 1994).

Come to set us free, St Thomas More Centre, (OCP: Portland 1987).

Holy is God St Thomas More Centre, (OCP: Portland 1988).

Jubilate Deo, (Catholic Truth Society: London 1979).

Music for the Mass, ed. Geoffrey Boulton Smith, (Geoffrey Chapman: London 1985).

Music for the Mass 2, ed. Geoffrey Boulton Smith and Christopher McCurry, (Geoffrey Chapman: London 1993).

Praise be to Christ, St Thomas More Group, (OCP: Portland 2003).

Psalms of Prayer, Protest and Praise John Bell, (Wild Goose Publications: Glasgow).

Psalm Songs (Volumes 1–3) ed. David Ogden and Alan Smith, (Geoffrey Chapman: London 1998).

Rejoice 'n' Sing 1 Jo Boyce, Christopher Rolinson, Mike Stanley, (CJM Music: Birmingham 1996).

Songs and Prayers from Taizé, (Continuum: London 2002).

Songs of the Spirit 3 ed. Damian Lundy, (Kevin Mayhew: Stowmarket 1987).

Veni Emmanuel ed Stephen Dean, (Decani Music: Mildenhall 2001).

We are your people, St Thomas More Center, (OCP: Portland 1986).

ACKNOWLEDGEMENTS

The Liturgy Office is grateful to the following people for the assistance they provided: Pauline Clarke, Robin Gibbons, Alan Griffiths, Anna Hawke.

This volume does not contain ready-to-use liturgies but, as explained on page 20, provides a resource for local celebrations. Most groups will require a leaflet and both in the text and on the accompanying CD-ROM resources are provided to facilitate the production of leaflets. This will involve the use of copyright texts and music. The purchase of this volume in itself does not give the right to re-use all the material it contains.

Following the guidance of the Bishops' Conference on producing leaflets for liturgy it is assumed that the leaflet will not normally include ministerial texts (prayers, readings etc.) unless they are necessary to cue a congregational response.

The publisher acknowledges permission to reproduce copyright material in this book. Every effort has been made to trace copyright holders and obtain permission. If there are any omissions we apologise and will include suitable acknowledgements in any future edition.

80–82   © Abbaye de Tamié, Plancherine 73200, Albertville, Savoie, France.

55, 60–62, 65, 68, 69, 100, 102, 134, 135   © Ampleforth Abbey Trustees, Ampleforth Abbey, York YO62 4EN.

39, 44, 51, 52, 170   © Ateliers et Presses de Taizé, 71250 Taizé Communauté, France.

77, 84, 85   © Downside Abbey Trustees, Stratton-on-the-Fosse, Bath BA3 4RH.

154   © Timothy Dudley-Smith, in Europe (including UK and Ireland) and in all territories not controlled by the Hope Publishing Company, USA. All rights reserved.

114, 115, 121   © 1993, Bernadette Farrell and Owen Alstott. Published by OCP Publications, 5536 N.E. Hassalo, Portland, OR 97213, USA. All rights reserved. Used with permission.

64, 67, 78, 79, 96, 97, 100–102   © 2006 Martin Foster. Published by Decani Music, Oak House, 70 High Street, Brandon, Suffolk IP27 0AU

49*, 50*, 166   © GIA Publications Inc, 7404 S.Mason Avenue, Chicago, IL 60638, USA.

40, 45, 55, 60, 61, 64, 65, 70–73, 76–81, 84, 86, 87, 90, 92, 107–111, 118, 119 Psalm texts from *The Psalms: A New Translation* © 1963, 1986, 1993 The Grail (England). Reprinted by permission of HarperCollins Publishers Ltd, 77–85 Fulham Palace Road, Hammersmith, London W6 8JB.

98, 99, 102, 108, 109, 118   © Kevin Mayhew Ltd, Buxhall, Stowmarket, Suffolk IP14 3BW.

112, 113, 120, 170   © 1984, 1991, OCP Publications, 5536 N.E. Hassalo, Portland, OR 97213, USA. All rights reserved. Used with permission.

47, 48   Material from *Celebrating Common Prayer* © 1992, The Society of St Francis, Hilfield Friary, Dorchester, Dorset DT2 7BE. Used by permission.

42, 43, 52   © 1988, Christopher Walker. Published by OCP Publications, 5536 N.E. Hassalo, Portland, OR 97213, USA. All rights reserved. Used with permission.

136, 137   arrangement by D Higgins © Westminster Cathedral Music Department, 42 Francis Street, London SW1P 1QW.

38, 51   John L Bell © 1995 WGRG, Iona Community, Glasgow G2 3DH.

FULL LIST OF CONTENTS

⊙ indicates inclusion of material on CD-ROM

INDEX OF FIRST LINES
including Index of Assembly Editions

Where two page numbers are indicated, the first is for Assembly Edition music, and the second for full music. Entries marked § contain text only.